TUPE: A Practical Guide

Other titles available from Law Society Publishing:

Civil Litigation Handbook
Edited by John Peysner

Conditional Fees: A Survival Guide
Edited by Fiona Bawdon, Michael Napier and Gordon Wignall

Conveyancing Handbook
Frances Silverman

Criminal Defence
Roger Ede and Anthony Edwards

Elderly Client Handbook
Gordon R. Ashton with Anne Edis

Employment Law Handbook
Daniel Barnett and Henry Scrope

Environmental Law Handbook
Trevor Hellawell

Immigration Advice at the Police Station
Rosie Brennan

Probate Practitioner's Handbook
Edited by Lesley King

Wrongful Dismissal
Julian Yew

All books from Law Society Publishing can be ordered through good bookshops or direct from our distributors, Marston Book Services, by telephone 01235 465656 or email law.society@marston.co.uk (please confirm prices including postage before ordering). For further information or a catalogue, call our editorial and marketing office on 020 7316 5876.

TUPE: A PRACTICAL GUIDE

Gill Sage

The Law Society

ISBN 1–85328–815–2

Published in 2002 by the Law Society
113 Chancery Lane, London WC2A 1PL

Typeset by J&L Composition, Filey, North Yorkshire
Printed by Anthony Rowe Ltd, Chippenham, Wilts

Acknowledgements

Dedicated to GRJ Sage, with love.

With heartfelt thanks to Claire 'the Fish' Fisher for her help and assistance in the writing and production of this book.

Thank you to my friends Sally, Jaq, and Sue, without you it would not have been possible.

To Kevin, the Ogre, with love.

Contents

Table of cases

Table of statutes

Table of statutory instruments and European legislation

CHAPTER 1

Background to TUPE

1.1 PREVIOUS LEGAL POSITION

Introduction

Under common law, the transfer of a business previously had the effect of automatically terminating all contracts of employment, with dismissals resulting. This gave dismissed employees the chance to claim wrongful or unfair dismissal or a redundancy payment against the transferor alone (see *Nokes* v. *Doncaster Amalgamated Collieries Limited* [1940] AC 1014, HL).

If the transferor was insolvent or had sold all the assets of the company or if dissolution had taken place, dismissed employees would have no remedy against the employer. Their claims would go uncompensated, with the exception of claims against the state for redundancy payments in the event of the company's insolvency. The employee's only other claim would be based upon the law of contract, and unless privity of contract could be shown, the employee would not be able to take action against the purchaser or transferee of a business. It was therefore relatively easy for businesses to avoid responsibility to employees by changing their legal structure. The Transfer of Undertakings (Protection of Employment) Regulations, SI 1981/1794 (the TUPE regulations) were introduced to protect the interests of employees who were detrimentally affected by the sale or transfer of a business. They allowed the courts to look behind legal structures to protect the rights of employees.

The TUPE regulations were drafted widely without recourse to restrictive definitions or interpretative guidance as it was recognised that it was possible to change business structures discretely in order to avoid claims by employees in respect of contractual and statutory rights. Transfers such as sales, leasebacks, contracting out, grants of leases and licences and changes in the management structure of a company have all been held to be relevant transfers that fall within the ambit of TUPE. The TUPE provisions have been interpreted widely with what is called the 'purposive approach' in order to give effect to the spirit, intention and purpose of the regulations. As new methods are devised to avoid TUPE, so the law seems to rise to meet the challenge. This is why the law in this area appears to be in a constant state of development: as businesses adopt different structures to avoid the impact of the regulations, so the courts employ a broad brush interpretation to restore their effect.

Looking at court decisions over the past ten years, there appears to be a trend from which rules can be derived. This book attempts to give guidance on the direction in which decisions regarding the application of TUPE are moving in order that the best advice can be provided to clients, whether they be transferors, transferees or employees.

The European Directive and its historical roots

The stated intention of the Acquired Rights Directive (77/187 EEC) (the Directive) was 'to provide for the protection of employees in the event of a change in the employer, in particular, to ensure that their rights [were] safeguarded'. This was to be achieved by providing that, in the event of a transfer of an undertaking, business or part of a business to another as a result of a legal transfer, merger or other disposition, the transferor's legal rights and obligations arising from a contract of employment or from an employment relationship existing on the date of the transfer 'shall by reason of such transfer, be transferred to the Transferee'. This meant that an employee's contract of employment would be automatically taken over by the transferee employer as if it had originally been made with the transferee. The period of continuous service with the transferor employer counted as continuous service with the transferee. In this way, the Directive sought to provide protection to employees caught up in a business transfer by providing that their contracts transferred across and were enforceable against the transferee.

Political background to the implementation of TUPE

The TUPE regulations were introduced to implement the provisions of the Directive into domestic jurisdiction. Implementation of the Directive was required within two years of 1977, but the UK delayed introducing the measures until it became the subject of infraction proceedings. Even when the TUPE regulations were introduced in the Commons, the lack of enthusiasm for them was startling. It was as a result of this lack of enthusiasm that the regulations and Directive differed so much, leaving scope for a wide interpretation as a result of imprecise and lax drafting. As a direct result of this reluctance the TUPE regulations have been amended on many occasions by subsequent legislation to bring them into line with the spirit and intention of the Directive. The Directive has also been amended, most recently on 12 March 2001, and it is now Council Directive 2001/23/EC (see Appendix 1). However, all references in this section are to the 1977 Directive unless otherwise stated.

Differences between the Directive and TUPE

The differences that were apparent between the Directive and TUPE were as follows.

Voluntary and involuntary transfers

The TUPE regulations applied to transfers that were both voluntary and involuntary, whereas the Directive applied only to voluntary transfers. This was the only area in which the regulations had a wider scope than the Directive. The regulations therefore applied to public sector transfers whereas the Directive did not. However, the change introduced on the 12 March 2001 by Council Directive 2001/23/EC extended the Directive's jurisdiction to the public sector. Article 1 of that Directive now confirms that it applies to

> [p]ublic and private undertakings engaged in economic activities whether or not they are operating for gain. An administrative reorganisation of public administrative authorities, or the transfer of administrative functions between public administrative authorities, is not a transfer within the meaning of the Directive.

It is now, therefore, clear that the Directive specifically excludes only public administrative functions. But if the public function is an economic activity, e.g. refuse collection, transport or a service provision, will the Directive be deemed to apply?

Scope of employment

Article 3 of the Directive states that not only shall the transferor's rights and obligations arising from the contract of employment transfer, but also its rights 'from an employment relationship'. It therefore appears that art. 3 is wider than TUPE reg. 5, which seems to limit the effect of the transferor's rights to those in connection with 'a contract of employment'.

Dismissals for economic, technical or organisational reasons

Article 4 provides that the transfer of an undertaking shall not of itself constitute grounds for dismissal by the transferor or the transferee. This does not stand in the way of dismissals that may take place for 'economic, technical or organisational reasons entailing changes in the workforce' (ETO).

Regulation 8 is drafted in the negative, saying that a dismissal is automatically unfair if the transfer or a reason connected with a transfer is the reason for dismissal. However, the dismissal will not be automatically unfair if the employer has the ETO defence. The employer must, however, show that the ETO arises as a consequence and in connection with the transfer.

In *D'urso* v. *Ercole Marelli Elettromeccanica Generale SpA (in special administration)* (C-362/89) [1992] IRLR 136, ECJ, the Advocate General did not share the view that the Directive permitted any dismissal for an ETO. He felt that it expressly prohibited dismissals when they were the result of the transfer of an undertaking. Only dismissals which would have been carried out in any case fell within the exclusion. This case suggested that there had been a major misjudgement in the implementation of the Directive.

However, in the case of *Trafford* v. *Sharpe and Fisher (Building Supplier) Ltd* [1994] IRLR 325, EAT, it was held that there was no obvious discrepancy between the Directive and the TUPE regulations. While the purposive approach required the safeguarding of employees' rights 'as far as possible', art. 4 of the Directive acknowledged that the rights of employees not to be dismissed should not stand in the way of dismissals for an ETO. In such circumstances, the rights of employees were to be outweighed by the economic reasons for dismissal.

Commercial ventures

When the TUPE regulations were drafted, a form of words was inserted into the definition which excluded those transfers 'which were not in the nature of a commercial venture'. The Directive contained no such words. This form of words was reversed with the landmark case of *Dr Sophie Redmond Stichting* v. *Bartol* (C-29/91) [1992] IRLR 366, where it was held that the transfer of a subsidy away from one foundation to another was a transfer. It was therefore clear that the Directive applied to non-commercial organisations.

Section 33 of the Trade Union Reform and Employment Rights Act 1993 amended TUPE reg. 2(1) by deleting the reference to undertakings 'which were not in the nature of a commercial venture'.

Consultation

Article 7(2) of the Directive provides that consultations with employees' representatives should take place with a view to seeking agreement. There was no parallel right in the TUPE regulations until the Trade Union Reform and Employment Rights Act 1993 amended them. The UK was the subject of proceedings by the Commission for failing to fulfil its obligations under the Directive by not providing a mechanism for employees' representatives to be consulted.

This failure was rectified by the passing of the Collective Redundancies and the Transfer of Undertakings (Protection of Employment) (Amendment) Regulations 1995 (SI 1995/2587). This legislation extended the duty to inform and consult with elected representatives where there was no recognised trade union. It also allowed employers to consult with elected representatives rather than with the recognised trade union.

A subsequent amendment by the 1999 regulations then took away the employer's right to consult with elected representatives rather than with the representatives from recognised trade unions. Now employers must, where there is a recognised trade union, consult with all trade unions and appropriate representatives. However, even though the original regulations introduced an obligation to inform and consult, they also introduced an escape route for those who failed to inform and consult. This was where the employer could show 'special circumstances' under reg. 10(7). No such defence appears in the Directive.

Pensions and benefits

Article 3 of the Directive does not cover '[e] mployees' rights to old age, invalidity or survivors' benefit under supplementary company or inter-company pension schemes outside the statutory social security schemes'. TUPE reg. 7 went wider to include '[a]ny rights of employees arising under or in relation to an occupational pension scheme'.

5

This definition was held to be too broad as it could include payment for voluntary severance and redundancy payments. The Trade Union Reform and Employment Rights Act 1993 therefore amended reg. 7 to bring it into line with the Directive by providing that any provisions of an occupational pension scheme which did not relate to benefits for old age, invalidity or survivor's benefit should be treated as not being part of the scheme. This ensured that reg. 7 would only apply to the occupational pensions part of any company scheme. It would not apply to parts of the scheme that related to non-pension benefits which were, therefore, capable of transferring.

Choice of employment

In the case of *EC Commission* v. *Belgium* [1988] 2 MLR 265, ECJ, it was said that the implementation of the Directive should not diminish employees' existing rights in any way. The common law right to decline to transfer did not appear either in the Directive or in the TUPE regulations. The only right to 'object' was under art. 4(2), which confirmed that if an employee terminated the employment relationship because of a '[s]ubstantial change in working conditions to the employee's detriment', the employer should be regarded as having been responsible for the termination of the relationship. This preserved an employee's right to claim constructive dismissal and was reflected in reg. 5(5). There was concern that the TUPE regulations and the Directive were too restrictive of employees, as an assumption had been made that all employees would wish to transfer. No account was taken of the fact that some employees might not wish to work for the transferee and there appeared to be no mechanism under the Directive or the regulations for the employee to elect not to transfer. Employees were assumed to be sold with the business as part of the assets. The provisions that had been introduced to protect employment, but which placed employees in a situation that appeared to diminish their rights to choose for whom they wished to work, were felt to be against the spirit and intention of the Directive.

In response to the European case of *Katsikas* v. *Konstantinides* [1993] IRLR 179, ECJ an amendment to the TUPE regulations was introduced by the Trade Union Reform Employment Rights Act 1993 which provided that any employee could object to becoming employed by the transferee, in which event he or she would not transfer with the undertaking. This left employees with no remedy if they chose to object, as they were not under these circumstances treated as having been dismissed by the transferor; therefore they had no rights upon termination of their contract. This amendment is reg. 5(4A) and 5(4B), which preserves the right of employees to choose whom they work for.

How have the inconsistencies been reconciled?

When there have been inconsistencies between the Directive and the TUPE regulations, two mechanisms have been adopted by the judicial systems to reconcile them. First, when the employer is an 'emanation of the state', i.e. the employee works for a government department, local authority or a quango or in certain prescribed employment, the Directive has a direct effect (see *Francovich* v. *Italian Republic* (C-6/90) [1992] IRLR 84). Second, the Directive can be used as an aid to the construction of TUPE in order to clear up any inconsistencies. The most famous example of this latter approach is *Litster* v. *Forth Dry Dock and Engineering Co. Ltd* [1989] IRLR 161, where the House of Lords adopted the 'purposive approach' by implying the words '[o]r would have been so employed if he had not been unfairly dismissed in the circumstances described in regulation 8 (1)' to prevent employees who had been dismissed by the transferor shortly before the transfer from being denied the protection of the TUPE regulations. There are many examples throughout this book where the purposive approach has been adopted in the UK national courts.

1.2 THE TUPE REGULATIONS AND THEIR IMPLEMENTATION

Introduction

The TUPE regulations are very brief and they contain few definitions to assist with interpretation. UK domestic courts have often been faced with the question of whether they will apply to a particular set of facts. If they do apply, employee rights will be preserved as against any transferee who acquires the business. The employee will then have jurisdiction to apply to the employment tribunal to complain of unfair dismissal or breach of contract against the transferee. If the regulations do not apply, employees will have no claim against the transferee of a business – their only claim will be against the dismissing transferor.

For the TUPE regulations to apply the employee must prove that there has been a 'relevant transfer' of an 'undertaking' and that the transfer is of an 'economic entity'. None of these terms is subject to clear and unequivocal interpretation in the regulations and they have therefore been the subject of judicial interpretation through case law in the UK courts and in the European Court of Justice.

In order to advise a client whether the TUPE regulations or the Directive apply to a particular transaction, it must first be established that a relevant transfer has taken place. This is the first hurdle to overcome and is pivotal for the subsequent advice to be delivered. The first part of this book therefore provides an outline of the case law in connection with the question of what amounts to a relevant transfer under the TUPE regulations.

So who benefits from TUPE?

Diverse opinions are held of the benefits that the Directive and the TUPE regulations bring to the commercial world. Commercial lawyers tend to view TUPE as a problem to overcome, an unnecessary intrusion upon the rights of their clients to sell or transfer their businesses as they wish, unencumbered by consideration for the interests of employees. The regulations are often not given priority in negotiations and are often not referred to in agreements for sale. Often, little or no thought is given to the obligations upon the parties to inform and consult, commercial lawyers taking the view that negotiations are confidential to the parties and that price sensitivities are paramount.

Employment lawyers, on the other hand, hold different views on the value of TUPE to their clients. The regulations provide valuable protection for employees, preventing any dismissals on the grounds of a transfer. If a dismissal does take place, it will be deemed to be automatically unfair, placing the burden of proof upon the employer to show a defence was available.

If an employment lawyer were acting for an employer in a transfer situation, guidance would have to be given as to the likely applicability of TUPE and the need to provide for indemnities and cross-indemnities in respect of any claim submitted by an employee as a result of the transfer. A provision would have to be made for employees to be informed and consulted throughout the negotiations. Ensuring that this obligation is adequately performed will be a growth area for lawyers in both the employment and commercial fields. Failure to inform and consult not only leaves both the transferor and the transferee exposed to the likelihood of claims but it also prevents the possibility of negotiating a way forward with employees who wish to transfer and the identification of those who do not. If employees indicate that they do not wish to transfer, they will not be compelled to transfer and will either remain with the transferor or be treated as if they have unreservedly resigned. If they are treated as if they have resigned from the business their only claim will be against the transferor in respect of any fundamental breach of contract. The employee may wish to remain with the transferor; if this view is expressed it needs to be explored in order to assess the possible liabilities to the business in terms of the future wages bill and the risk of future litigation.

The TUPE regulations provide substantial benefits to certain types of employee who are caught up in the transfer of a business. The case law in this book tends to focus on employees performing largely blue-collar, unskilled or semi-skilled functions, such as cleaning, security, catering and other functions within the service industry. These employees are usually at the lower end of the earnings scale. It is because of their perceived status (or lack of it) within an organisational structure that they tend to be forgotten when a business transfer takes effect. Their contribution and the value of their skills to the business are considered to be unimportant or replaceable, and as a result they are often ignored or overlooked when a business is sold or transferred. The TUPE regulations have gone some way to redress this problem by giving these employees a right to be informed, consulted and considered when a business is being sold or transferred. The regulations have provided real and quantifiable power precisely to those employees who were previously powerless, by giving them the right, backed up by an enforceable legal remedy, to be included in the process. To that extent TUPE has been a success.

Very little case law in this book deals with the transfer of senior executives' contracts. This is because the TUPE regulations do not apply where the contract is not transferred by reason of the transfer but is renegotiated by the employee and the transferee independently, as would be the case with most senior employees. The regulations do not in any way fetter the freedom of parties of equal bargaining power to renegotiate their contractual terms in a mutually beneficial way. However, employers should be aware that if they attempt to impose new terms on senior employees as a result of a transfer, these changes are likely to be void. This will then entitle employees to treat themselves as constructively dismissed and discharged from all liabilities and duties under the contract, including those in respect of restrictive covenants.

As the TUPE regulations will most probably apply to employees in the lower earnings bracket, it may be prudent to consider the cost to the business of the employees transferring. The transferee should assume that employees will transfer and build this in to the price of the business. The transferee must also be cautious of any dismissals that took place at a time reasonably proximate to the transfer; as the liability for those dismissals will transfer to the transferee, it will be necessary to consider getting indemnities from the transferor in respect of them. This cost should also be considered by the transferor in calculating the risk of litigation arising out of the transfer, including claims arising out of the failure to inform and consult and in respect of unfair dismissal. Any potential claim should then be covered by asking for indemnities from the transferee. These cross-indemnities will protect both buyer and seller from any claims that may arise and they give recognition to the fact that the TUPE regulations should have a pivotal place in transfers of undertakings.

If a transfer is always handled on the understanding that the TUPE regulations will apply and that all employees will transfer, at the information and consultation stage employees may take the decision not to transfer and choose to leave voluntarily. Employees who do decide to transfer may decide later on that the new business is not for them and then resign. It is not always the case that a transferee will be stuck with a workforce that it does not want. Change often induces employees to take the initiative and seek new employment after a transfer. It is also important to remember that an employer is always entitled to dismiss for a fair reason within the Employment Rights Act 1996 (as long as that reason is not connected with the transfer). If an employee turns out to be incapable on the grounds of competence or ill health or guilty of gross misconduct, these will be fair reasons to dismiss.

If, however, a transferor wrongly reaches the conclusions that, on the facts, TUPE does not apply, and all the employees are dismissed in order to sell the business unencumbered, the risks to both the transferor and transferee will be great in terms of the time and valuable resources spent on fighting employment tribunal claims. The risk to the transferee may be greater in terms of adverse publicity and negative feedback from staff and customers. Complying with the spirit and intention of the regulations therefore appears to be the most prudent route to follow. This book attempts to show why and how this can be done and to set out the most pragmatic steps to take to achieve the stated objective of according with the TUPE regulations.

The book is arranged in chronological order of the steps that are likely to be taken in connection with a relevant transfer under the regulations. At the end of each chapter is a section offering practical advice that should be taken into consideration by the transferor, the transferee or the employee. It is hoped that this will provide a logical and user-friendly approach to a subject that appears to provide more questions than answers.

CHAPTER 2

Component parts of a transfer

It is clear from the overview in Chapter 1 that the Directive was enacted in 1977 with the admirable objective of 'safeguarding employees' rights when the business in which they work changes hands between employers'.

When the TUPE regulations came into force in 1981 to give effect to the Directive in the UK, it was evident that there were real differences between the two documents, resulting in various statutory amendments to the regulations and clarification to their meaning via case law. The Directive was subsequently revised in 1998 and a consolidated version was adopted in 2001. The 1998 version gave all member states the flexibility to tailor their implementing measures to their particular national circumstances. The UK's implementing measures are, of course, the TUPE regulations and they are now under a detailed review by way of a public consultation exercise (see Appendix 4). It is likely that many of the uncertainties raised in this book will be clarified when the new regulations are published.

In this section we look at where the law stands at present. All references to the Directive are to the 2001 consolidated version (see Appendix 1) and all references to the TUPE regulations are to the 1981 regulations as amended (see Appendix 3).

As a necessary pre-condition of the TUPE regulations applying to a transaction, it must be shown that there is a 'relevant transfer' of an 'economic entity'. The regulations are short and provide very little guidance on how to determine whether they apply to a particular transaction. The case law is not always as consistent and helpful as might be hoped. European Court of Justice (ECJ) decisions give rulings on the interpretation of the Directive from other European jurisdictions. These are binding judicial rulings on the Directive itself, and thus on the TUPE regulations which implement it in domestic UK jurisdiction.

In this section of the book, the main definitions are looked at in the context of the developing case law to establish what criteria are necessary for the transfer of an undertaking to exist.

2.1 DEFINITIONS

The following definitions are used in the TUPE regulations.

Employee

An employee is any individual who works for another person whether under a contract of service or apprenticeship or otherwise. This definition will extend to anyone who works in any capacity except that of a genuinely independent contractor or casual worker. In order to obtain some clarification on the issue of who can look to the TUPE regulations for protection in the event of a relevant transfer, we need to look at art. 2 of the Directive. This confirms that an employee is any person who is protected as an employee under national employment law. This definition has been subject to further clarification under art. 2(2), which confirms that member states should not exclude employees from the scope of the Directive (or its implementing regulations) solely because they

(a) work part time;
(b) work under a fixed term contract;
(c) are temporary workers.

It is clear, therefore, that UK domestic employment law needs to be interpreted in the light of the provisions of the Directive. It is likely that all of the above employees who have acquired one year's continuous service will be able to enjoy the protection offered by the TUPE regulations.

In order for an employee to acquire the protection of the regulations it must be shown that there is a contract of employment. This presupposes that the contract contains an element of mutuality of obligation in order for it to bring itself within the definition of an employment contract. It is likely that those employed under casual contracts which do not have the requisite mutuality of obligation would not transfer under the regulations as their contracts would not be contracts of service 'or otherwise'. In the cases of *Carmichael* v. *National Power* [2000] IRLR 43, HL and *Stevedoring Haulage Services Ltd* v. *Fuller and Others* (CA, 9 May 2001) the Court of Appeal decided that where a contract failed to show the requisite mutuality of obligations, a contract of employment could not be implied.

However, one also needs to be suspicious of any relationship that appears not to be one of employment by virtue of the fact that tax and national insurance are not deducted but are paid by the contractor as if it were a self-employed person. Although this evidence is taken into consideration, it is not conclusive in showing that a contractor is indeed self-employed. The courts will look at all the facts of the relationship, as was seen in the case of *Reid* v. *North West Ceilings Ltd T/A Shopspec* (EAT, 2 April 2001).

In establishing whether particular staff are protected under TUPE, all those who are or could be employees need to be included. Self-employed persons could be deemed to be employees if their work was sufficiently integrated into the business to conform to the control test, as seen in the case of *Ready Mixed Concrete (SE) Ltd* v. *The Minister of Pensions and National Insurance* [1968] 2 QB 487. If there is doubt it may be prudent to treat all those who work regular hours as employees.

It is also necessary to be aware that agency staff can be deemed to be employees and, therefore, protected by TUPE. The case of *Motorola Ltd* v. *Davidson and Melville Craig Group Ltd* [2001] IRLR 4, EAT involved an agency worker, D, working under a contract for services. After two years of continuous work for Motorola, D was suspended, disciplined and then dismissed. He sued Motorola for unfair dismissal. Motorola argued that D was not entitled to pursue a claim against it as it had not exercised a sufficient degree of control over him to give rise to an employment relationship. The EAT held that Motorola had a sufficient degree of control over D to amount to an employment relationship. That control was held to include:

(a)   working on Motorola's site;
(b)   receiving instructions from Motorola's employees;
(c)   using Motorola's tools;
(d)   wearing the company uniform;
(e)   having to book holidays to fall in with other staff;
(f)   having to raise grievances with Motorola's employees;
(g)   being suspended by Motorola's staff;
(h)   being dismissed by Motorola's staff.

The relationship was held to be an employment relationship, even though D could, at any time, have chosen not to work for Motorola without breaching the contract and the agency could have removed him from the site at any time. As Motorola had practical control over D this amounted to an employment relationship.

Undertaking

Undertaking 'includes any trade or business'. This has extended to any non-commercial undertaking since the case of *Dr Sophie Redmond Stichting* v. *Bartol* (C-29/92) [1992] IRLR 366.

Relevant transfer

Under art. 1 of the Directive, a transfer is defined as:

> a Transfer of an economic entity which retains its identity, meaning an organised grouping of resources, which has the objective of pursuing an economic activity, whether or not that activity is central or an ancillary . . .

The Directive will now apply to public and private transfers when these concern entities engaging in economic activities.

The TUPE regulations state that a relevant transfer is a '[t]ransfer from one person to another of an undertaking situated immediately before the transfer in the UK or part of one which is so situate'. The regulations will apply whether the transfer is effected by sale or by some other disposition or operation of law. No definition is supplied save for the words 'a Transfer to which the Regulations apply'. A transfer of assets alone, or a sale of shares, will not amount to a relevant transfer but excluding these two exceptions, most legal transfers will amount to a relevant transfer under TUPE.

2.2 IDENTIFYING A RELEVANT TRANSFER

In order for the TUPE regulations to apply, individuals seeking to rely on their provisions must show that they are employees who are protected under UK law. It must then be shown that there is a relevant transfer of an undertaking. The following tests have been devised by the courts in an attempt to give clear guidance as to when the regulations will apply to a transfer.

The going concern test

In order to decide whether a business has been transferred, a judicial test called the 'going concern' test was formulated. The ECJ considered this at length and refined it by looking at whether the business retained its identity after the transfer. The ECJ gave clear guidance to all domestic jurisdictions that the method for deciding whether an undertaking had transferred was to look at whether it had retained its identity and this involved taking account of a number of factors. This guidance given by the ECJ is adopted by national courts when deciding whether the transfer of an undertaking has taken place. *Spijkers* v. *Gebroeders Benedik Abattoir CV* (C-24/85) [1986] 2 CMLR 296, ECJ does not deal with contracting out but its relevance was endorsed in the case of *RCO Support Services Limited* v. *Unison* (CA, 12 April 2002), where it was held that it was necessary to determine whether what had been sold was an economic entity which was still in existence, and this would be apparent from the fact that the operation was actually being continued or had been taken over by the new employer within the same economic or similar activity.

In order to decide whether there is a transfer under the Directive or TUPE, the following matters must be considered:

(a)   the type of undertaking involved;
(b)   whether there was a transfer of assets;
(c)   the value of intangible assets;
(d)   whether and how many staff are taken on;
(e)   the transfer of customers;
(f)   similarity of activities before and after the transfer;
(g)   the duration of any interruption of services.

In an old pre-Directive case, it was felt that the simple approach would be of some assistance in answering the basic question 'does the business remain the same business in different hands?' (as per Lord Denning in *Lloyd* v. *Brassey* [1969] 2QB 98, CA).

The TUPE regulations will therefore apply to:

• sales of businesses;
• mergers and acquisitions;
• granting of leases;
• franchises, licences, concessions and grants;
• contracting out.

But the TUPE regulations do not apply to:

• share sales and transfers;
• asset sales alone;
• undertakings not situated in the UK;
• transfers of a ship;
• employees located overseas;
• independent contractors or partners in a business.

The definition of what is an undertaking and what is a relevant transfer contained in the Directive or the TUPE regulations is not precise, and it is for this reason that clarification has developed via case law. The courts have been free to interpret each set of facts before them according to a very wide set of criteria, which have no supporting guidelines. It is for this reason that there can be no certainty as to what is an undertaking and when a relevant transfer that attracts the protection offered by the regulations takes place.

Does the business retain its identity?

The next test to be developed was whether the business retained its identity. Whether advice is being offered to a transferor, or transferee or employee affected by the transfer of an undertaking, a view must be taken at an early stage of whether TUPE applies to the transaction or the series of transactions. It will always be safer to begin with the view that the regulations do apply. On the very worst scenario, the client should be advised to take steps to inform, consult and then perhaps to accommodate the staff employed in the undertaking, either by arranging for them to transfer with the sale of a business or for staff to be taken on when the business is purchased. If no staff are to be transferred, the job of the legal adviser may simply be to negotiate indemnities for the benefit of the transferee client. Failure to understand the full implications of TUPE and to advise the transferee accordingly could be expensive for the client. Those costs could be substantial in terms of employment tribunal claims, legal costs, adverse publicity and the disruption to the business. Even the transfer of a function can be deemed to be a relevant transfer under TUPE. A case on the Directive in the ECJ, *Rask and Christensen* v. *ISS Kantineservice A/S* (C-209/91) [1993] IRLR 133, clarified this point, and guided the UK national courts on their interpretation of the UK regulations.

Here Philips contracted out the running of its staff canteen to ISS for a fixed monthly fee. No assets transferred to ISS, it simply took over the employment and management of staff. It was held in this case that the critical question was 'whether the business retained its identity'. There was enough evidence to support the fact of a transfer as ISS took over the obligations of employer in respect of this function.

Factors to be taken into consideration include what happens to stock, premises, staff and also what happens to other assets such as copyrights, trademarks, patents and goodwill. These can all be taken into account but none is conclusive. The Directive has been interpreted widely but in UK domestic jurisdiction the nature of the interpretation has been difficult to predict, possibly as a result the loose drafting of the TUPE regulations and the government's own reluctance to incorporate the Directive fully into UK domestic legislation. This can best be seen in the following cases where few, if any, assets transferred.

Wren v. *Eastbourne Borough Council and UK Waste Control Limited* [1993] IRLR 425, EAT involved a local authority contracting out its waste disposal services under compulsory competitive tendering (CCT). Some employees were taken on and those who were not were dismissed. The dismissed employees claimed unfair dismissal. It was held that there was a transfer of an undertaking even though no assets were transferred, no goodwill was transferred and there were no outstanding contracts. Claims for unfair dismissal therefore succeeded.

In *Porter* v. *Queens Medical Centre (Nottingham University Hospital)* [1993] IRLR 486, QBD the defendant was a public sector employer who made new arrangements for the supply of paediatric services as a result of which two consultants lost their posts and claimed that their contracts had been transferred to the new employer. As they worked for an employer which was in the public sector and, therefore, an emanation of the state, they were entitled to rely directly on the Directive. It was held that the Directive did apply to the transfer, as the objectives of the undertaking itself remained constant. However, the defendant succeeded in relying on the defence of an ETO for changing the workforce and thus defeated the consultants' claims.

Although in the case of *Dines* v. *Initial Healthcare Services* [1995] ICR 11, CA there was no transfer of assets, equipment or goodwill, the fact that the objectives of the undertaking remained the same allowed the courts to find that there had been a relevant transfer. This case was a second generation contracting out dispute. Originally Company A won a cleaning contract but when the contract was put out again Company B won the tender. Company B took on most of Company A's employees but on lower pay. The employees claimed unfair dismissal against both Company A and Company B. Although Company B did not purchase or take over any equipment or assets or any other materials, it was held there was still a transfer of an undertaking in line with the case of *Schmidt* v. *Spar- und Leihkasse der Früheren Ämter Bordesholm, Kiel und Cronshagen* (C-392/92) [1994] IRLR 302, [1995] ICR 237 where it was held that the transfer of cleaning duties of a single employee to a company providing those services at other premises of the employer constituted a transfer of an undertaking. In *Isle of Scilly Council* v. *Brintel Helicopters Limited* [1995] IRLR 6, EAT the facts of the case were that the council contracted out the management of the airport to Brintel between 1986 and 1990. In 1992 Brintel went into administration and five employees were made redundant. Three of the employees were then taken back by the council but on different and less favourable terms. All five employees brought proceedings either claiming unfair dismissal or that they were entitled to the same terms and conditions that they had previously enjoyed with Brintel. It was held that there had been a transfer of an undertaking. The question of whether the economic entity had retained its identity was supplemented by a second test of 'whether the job previously done by the employee was still in existence'. The EAT said that an economic entity could comprise merely activities and employees; tangible assets might therefore be unimportant or non-existent. The fact that there was no goodwill transfer because the old economic entity had come to an end did not, of itself, prevent TUPE from applying.

The test of the stable economic entity

Up until this point the way in which the case law was being developed was quite clear. Then problems began when decisions were made which appeared to go against the prevailing consensus that had been reached on the interpretation of the Directive and the TUPE regulations. The following cases indicated that a distinction needed to be drawn between a 'mere loss of a contract' and the transfer of a business. The Directive and the regulations could not apply to the transfer of one specific works contract. The ECJ decision in *Rygaard* v. *Dansk Arbejdsgiver Forening* (C-48/94) [1996] IRLR 51, ECJ is useful interpretative guidance on the issue of when contracts can fall outside the operation of the Directive. This interpretation will be adopted by the national courts as the *ratio* to be followed when deciding whether a transfer has taken place to which the Directive (and its implementing regulations) should apply.

In this case the main contractor, a firm of carpenters, subcontracted work to A. A's work was then subcontracted out to B for finishing off. It was agreed that B would refund to A the cost of materials and B took over two of A's apprentices. A was then wound up. One of the apprentices was then dismissed by B. The apprentice then brought proceedings for unfair and wrongful dismissal against B. It was held that the Directive did not apply. The ECJ took the view that what had to be transferred was 'a stable economic entity' and it was held that there could be no stable economic entity where the activity was limited to the carrying out of one specific works contract. It was confirmed that the decisive criterion for determining whether there had been a transfer was whether the business in question retained its identity. In order to ascertain this, one had to look at all the facts of the case and the *Spijkers* checklist, which was specifically referred to in this case.

The Directive's aim is to ensure, as far as possible, that the contract of employment or the employment relationship continues unchanged for the transferee. An employee must not be placed in a less favourable position solely as a result of the transfer.

Süzen v. *Zehnacker Gebaudereinigung GmbH Krankenhausservice* (C-13/95) [1997] IRLR 255, ECJ was a case that was brought under the Directive as the applicant worked for an emanation of the state. The matter was pursued to the ECJ and, therefore, the decision will be binding on our domestic jurisdiction. The case took the definition of a stable economic entity further. Mrs Suzen, a school cleaner, lost her job in a contracting out situation. She sought a declaration to the effect that the transfer had not terminated her contract and that the transferee company still employed her. ECJ approved all existing authorities such as *Dines*, *Dr Sophie Redmond* and *Schmidt* and re-affirmed the following:

(a)   that the decisive criterion was whether the entity in question retained its identity;

(b)   that the absence of a contractual link between the transferor and transferee was certainly not conclusive; and

(c)   that a transfer takes place, within the Directive (and thus the national regulations) if the economic entity retains its identity.

The ECJ decided that the Directive did not apply to this situation and reached two conclusions that appear to fly in the face of previous decisions, namely that:

(a)   an entity cannot be reduced to an activity entrusted to it. An entity comprises other factors such as its workforce, its management, the way in which the work is organised, its operating methods and operational resources; and

(b)   that the mere loss of a service contract to a competitor cannot by itself indicate the existence of a transfer under the Directive.

In this case the contractor did not take on any existing staff, tangible or intangible assets and so, the Directive was held not to apply on the above reasoning.

The case was reconciled with the case of *Dines*, because in *Dines* the contractor took on the existing staff and so the Directive applied. The ECJ reached the conclusion in *Suzen* that the parties could therefore control the application of the Directive in labour-intensive industries by deciding whether or not to take on a majority of the former contractor's workforce.

The ECJ also said in this case that it was 'for the national court to establish in the light of the foregoing interpretative guidance, whether a transfer ha[d] occurred'. There has been recent comment on the cases of *Suzen* in the case of *RCO Support Services Limited* v. *Unison* (CA, 12 April 2002), where Mummery LJ said that

> I agree that it has become clear from *Suzen* and later Judgments that the Court of Justice now interprets the Directive as setting limits to its application in contracting out cases which were not expressly identified in *Spijkers* or *Schmidt* and other earlier Judgments of the Court of Justice. In particular, the mere fact that the putative Transferee carries on the same services at the putative Transferor had done, does not, by itself, support the conclusion that an entity retains its identity. It is not correct to treat that single circumstance as determinative in favour of the transfer. Indeed, there may be no scope of the application of the Directive in a case where, although the same labour intensive activities are continued or the same services are supplied by a new contractor, none of the workforce has been carried on.

It may, therefore, be that *Suzen* may again be moving into favour in contracting out situations. It was for this reason that the conclusion was reached in the case of *Betts* v. *Brintel Helicopters Limited* [1997] IRLR 361, CA. Here Shell UK lost its helicopter services contract to KLM. KLM had all the assets necessary to provide the service, took none of the workforce and removed the operation from Beccles to Norwich. It was held that there was no transfer of undertaking. In the decision two types of undertakings were identified, those which were 'labour intensive', i.e. *Dines* types of transfer where the staff combined to engage in an activity which continued or was resumed with substantially the same staff after the transfer and, therefore, retained its identity in the hands of the transferee, and 'other types of undertakings'. The test to apply in this case was *Spijkers*, which was more wide ranging.

The issue of whether the TUPE regulations applied to the *Dines* type of transfer depended upon whether all, a majority or any of the employees transferred. This gave transferors and transferees an opportunity to control whether TUPE would apply by deciding not to take on any employees. However, the courts were concerned about this potential loophole and they went on to apply the purposive approach to the facts of *ECM (Vehicle Delivery Service) Ltd* v. *Cox* [1999] IRLR 559, CA. Employees were drivers and yardmen employed by A to deliver vehicles to X. In 1993 this contract was lost to B which decided not to take on any of A's employees, who were all dismissed. These employees bought unfair dismissal proceedings against B. All dismissals were found to be automatically unfair on the grounds of a relevant transfer. Not surprisingly, the employer B relied upon the cases of *Suzen* and *Betts* in its defence.

The EAT started by looking at the decision in *Schmidt* and comparing it with the decision in *Suzen*. The question was whether the employees were dedicated to the business to the extent that there would be no employment for them without the contract in question, thus distinguishing their position from that of a 'mere loss of a customer' situation. The employees' continued employment was dependent upon the continued existence of the service contract and therefore there was an economic entity which retained its identity after the transfer. The customers and the work taken on were essentially the same. Even though no staff were engaged, the economic entity was retained. The court emphasised the importance of making the 'necessary factual appraisal' as set out in *Spijkers* in order to determine whether the undertaking has continued and retained its identity in different hands.

The EAT went on to conclude that it would not, as a matter of policy, be permissible to use *Suzen* to evade the TUPE regulations. A purposive approach had to be taken to ensure that a transferee was not allowed to evade the obligation of the regulations by refusing to comply with them in the first place.

It is quite clear from the above decisions that the absence of transferring assets or workforce does not preclude the existence of a relevant transfer. All the factors of the case (as seen in *Spijkers*) must be taken into account.

The organised group of workers test

The problems associated in identifying whether a relevant transfer has taken place were considered from a different perspective in the cases of *Francisco Hernandez Vidal SA* v. *Gomez Perez, Santner* v. *Hoechst AG, Gomez Montana* v. *Claro Sol SA, Red Nacional de Ferrocarriles*

Espanoles (Rerife) (joined cases C-127/96 C-229/96 and C-74/97) [1999] IRLR 132 and *Sanchez Hidalgo v. Association de Servicios Aser and Sociedad Cooperativa Minerva, Ziemann* v. *Ziemann Sicherheit GmbH and Horst Bohn Sicherheitdienst* (joined cases C-173/96 and C-247/96) [1999] IRLR 136, ECJ which produced another variation of the test for a transfer of an undertaking. The cases involved contracted out situations of either taking a contract back in house or transferring it to another contractor. The decisions determined that the term 'economic activity' referred to an organised group of persons and assets enabling an economic activity which pursued a specific objective to be exercised, but did not require the economic activity to have tangible or intangible assets. They confirmed that a group of wage-earners who were permanently assigned to a common task, might, in the absence of other factors, amount to an economic activity. The decisions paid a lot of attention to what the undertaking comprised before the transfer and less to what happened afterwards, i.e. they looked at whether an economic activity was transferred rather than whether a 'major part of the workforce has been taken over' (*Suzen*). This shift in emphasis may be helpful in establishing a clear principle that the courts will apply when looking at whether there has been a relevant transfer. The dismissal of staff will not be an effective way of evading the Directive and its implementing regulations.

2.3 TIMING OF THE TRANSFER

This timing of the transfer was discussed in the case of *Celtec Ltd* v. *Astley and others* [2001] IRLR 788, EAT. In this case the transfer was deemed to be completed when the new employer was in actual occupation and control of the old business, as held in the case of *Teeside Times Limited* v. *Drury* [1980] ICR 338, CA. The transfer was held in this case to have been completed in September 1990.

The facts of the case were that the government set up training and enterprise councils (TECs) in 1989 to take over training from the Department for Education and Employment in order to reduce the number of civil servants. One civil servant, Astley, commenced work for a TEC on a three-year secondment in 1990. On 16 September 1991 the Secretary of State wrote to the chairman of the TEC setting out arrangements for TECs to become the employers of the staff before the fifth year of the operation. Civil servants were free to choose whether to take up appointments with the TECs or to return to the civil service.

In September 1993, Astley resigned from the civil service and took up a job with the TEC. He was given written particulars of employment which showed the date for continuous employment to be 1993. Astley and other employees similarly affected bought an action under the Employment Rights Act 1996, s.11, asking the tribunal to determine whether their continuous employment should include their previous service with the civil service.

It was held by the EAT that there was a transfer of an undertaking and that the transfer was complete when the employer was in actual occupation and control of the business. The transfer therefore took place in 1990, even though the consequences continued until 1996 as a result of the legal setting up of the TEC and the legal transfer, and the further six years for employees to have their employment transferred. The employees' continuity of service was broken when they resigned from the civil service in 1993 to take up employment with the TEC. When the transfer occurred, the secondee was employed by the transferor. When the employees resigned the transfer had already taken place and therefore they could not enjoy the benefit of continuous service under reg. 5 to include that which they had gained during their previous employment with the civil service.

2.4 DIRECTION IN 2000

By the year 2000 it seemed that the courts had established a direction with regard to relevant transfers. They had also started to take into account the intentions of the parties where attempts were made deliberately to avoid the effects of TUPE, as could can be seen in the case of *Lightways (Contractors) Ltd* v. *Associated Holdings Ltd* [2000] IRLR 247, Court of Session.

In a second round of competitive tendering, the local authority asked those who were on the tender list to state whether their bids were submitted on the basis that TUPE applied. The tender gave the tenderers the option of submitting alternative bids contingent upon whether the regulations applied or not. Lightways was successful and the bid that was accepted on the basis that TUPE applied. After winning the contract Lightways then sought to argue that the regulations did not apply and that it was not bound to give them effect. Lightways sought to argue that the intentions of the parties were an irrelevant factor in determining whether the regulations applied.

The tribunal took into account the fact that the tender had been made on the basis that the regulations did apply. The parties' intentions shed light on the nature of the transaction. It is clear from this case that the parties' intentions will be a factor to be taken into account and that the issue of avoidance may be relevant.

The next case has led to further confusion about whether the TUPE regulations will apply to labour-intensive transfers where there is no transfer of assets. The decision in *Whitewater Leisure Management Ltd* v. *Barnes and Others* [2000] IRLR 456, EAT appears to go back to *Suzen* and thereby causes further confusion as to when the TUPE regulations will apply.

Whitewater Leisure Group was responsible for managing a leisure centre. The contract expired and was subject to CCT. The contract reverted back to the local authority but without the six managers who had been involved with the operation. Of the core team of 14, only 7 transferred back to the local authority, not including the manager or two assistant managers. The other employees who did not transfer included part-time and casual staff. No tangible or intangible assets transferred over. It was held that in this case there was no transfer.

On appeal to the EAT it was held that the tribunal should ask two questions:

1. Is there a relevant and sufficiently identifiable economic entity, i.e. one that is stable and discrete or 'sufficiently structured and autonomous'? It was argued that this was not a stable or discrete entity because the management team who did not transfer were intricately bound up with Whitewater's other operations. It was argued that the entity was not discrete or that it was not transferred. If the entity did not include senior management then it could not be said to be stable or autonomous.

2. Was there a transfer of an undertaking? In order to decide this one had to look to the *Spijkers* guidelines. There can clearly be transfer even without significant assets being transferred. Where assets are transferred, this is likely to indicate the existence of a relevant transfer. However, this was a case of a labour-intensive undertaking. The issue was whether a majority of staff were taken on, or if only a minority were taken on, whether the skills of the minority outweighed the skills of the majority. If the entity did not include the senior management it could not be said that a major part of the workforce had transferred.

The case of *Whitewater* has again caused confusion as to when the TUPE regulations apply and has made it necessary to look back to

Suzen. In an attempt to clarify the situation, Lindsay J has given some clear guidance in the following cases in order to reconcile *Suzen* with *ECM* and other decisions.

The first case, *RCO Support Services Ltd and another* v. *UNISON and another* [2000] IRLR 624, concerned an NHS trust, which made the decision to phase out patient care in one hospital and transfer it to another. Three cleaners refused to take up offers of employment in the new hospital. Three chefs who were not redeployed by the trust were dismissed by reason of redundancy but were invited by the contractor at the transferee hospital, RCO, to apply for posts. Only one of the chefs was successful.

The court held that the core of the business moved from one hospital to another. It was a change of location for the same business but carried on by a different company (Initial carried out the cleaning in the closing hospital and RCO serviced the new hospital). There were no assets or goodwill to be transferred. An economic entity in the form of catering support transferred from the trust to RCO. Both the cleaners and the catering staff were economic entities that transferred and so the TUPE regulations applied. The following guidance was given on the status of the relevant case law on the TUPE regulations to date:

1. There can be an undertaking and a transfer of it even if neither significant assets nor a majority of the workforce moves.
2. All the facts of the transfer must be considered.
3. The factual appraisal of the case is for the employment tribunal to carry out.
4. The decisive criterion for determining whether a transfer has taken place is whether the business in question retains its identity in the hands of the new employer.
5. It is not decisive that a majority of the workforce is not transferred and this is also only one of the relevant criteria to be taken into account, with none alone being decisive. *ECM* v. *Cox* is the decision to follow as it was later in time than the case of *Betts* and in its judgment considered the decision of *Betts.*
6. *Spijkers* and *Schmidt* were still the authoritative decisions to follow when determining whether the business retained its identity.

In the second case, *Argyll Training Ltd* v. *Sinclair and another* [2000] IRLR 630, S was employed by B Company as a training adviser. B had a contract with Argyll Ltd (A) to provide training to local companies. S had sole responsibility for arranging training for employees with placement companies. A paid B. In 1998 B lost the contract with A and S was made redundant. A entered into contract with Argyll Training (AT) which enabled AT to take over all of B's placement trainees. AT took over 21 of the 32 placement trainees, S was not offered employment.

The court found that there had been a relevant transfer from B to A to AT even though there was no transfer of tangible assets and S was the only employee capable of being transferred. AT was carrying out the same duties as B and in practical terms they were indistinguishable. The undertaking had a separate income and identifiable outgoings and an arranged body of information, which included all the details of the trainees.

In the decision on this case Lindsay J (who also gave a powerful lead in the case of *RCO* above and *Cheesman* below) developed his approach to dealing with the case of *Suzen*:

1. The ECJ encouraged a breadth of approach when deciding whether an undertaking existed, so the employment tribunal was entitled to find that the training contract together with arrangements in place in connection with its performance amounted to an undertaking.

2. The fact that the undertaking consisted of one specific contract did not prevent it from being an undertaking. It was suggested that *Rygaard* was to be doubted and that its applicability should be restricted to its literal meaning to apply only to single specific contracts for building works. *Spijkers* and *Schmidt* were both referred to in the case of *Rygaard* and there was no indication that single contract undertakings were excluded from the application of the Directive or the regulations.

3. As was stated in *ECM*, *Suzen* could not be taken to have overruled the previous decision of the ECJ. *Schmidt* was therefore still good authority for the decisive consideration of whether the business in question (the economic entity) retained its identity, as indicated by the actual continuation or resumption of the same or similar activities.

4. Even if a transfer of assets was required, there was a body of intangible assets, namely, 'a convenient aggregation of relevant business information relating to the employer's placement business' which would justify the employment tribunal in finding that a requirement was met on the facts.

Lindsay J again used his common-sense purposive approach in the case of *Cheesman* v. *R Brewer Contracts Ltd* [2001] IRLR 144 where the maintenance for a housing stock was contracted out to Onyx in

1995. In 1998 a second round of tendering occurred and the contract was lost to Brewer. The staff were dismissed by Onyx and were not re-employed by Brewer. No assets, tangible or intangible, passed from Onyx to Brewer. The dismissed employees brought claims for unfair dismissal against Brewer. The employment tribunal applied *Suzen* and found that this was not a relevant transfer. The matter was then appealed to the EAT and it was held that:

1. The employment tribunal had erred in law by elevating the retention of the workforce into a decisive criterion rather than considering all the facts.
2. The tribunal also erred in failing to ask itself two separate questions: 'is there a stable economic entity?' And 'is there a relevant transfer of that entity?'
3. If the tribunal did not know what the entity was, they were likely to mislead themselves as to what had been transferred.

The EAT went on to analyse the relevant principles and considerations that could be applied from the cases of *Vidal*, *Sanchez Hidalgo*, *Allen* and from *ECM*. This case again put *Suzen* in its place by focusing on the more common-sense purposive approach. The principles that were formulated here were as follows.

In identifying an economic entity:

1. The stable economic activity must not be limited to one specific works contract.
2. It must be sufficiently structured or autonomous (this does not mean that it need have any significant assets).
3. An organised grouping of wage-earners who are specifically and permanently assigned to a common task may, in the absence of other factors of production, constitute an economic entity.
4. An activity itself is not enough. The identity of the entity comes from other factors such as the workforce or the management, the way in which the work is organised, the operating methods and, where appropriate, the operational resources available to it.

In identifying a transfer:

1. Has the entity retained its identity, has the operation been continued or resumed?
2. It is necessary to consider all the facts together to decide whether there has been a relevant transfer. No factor is to be considered in isolation.
3. The *Spijkers* criteria are to be considered as seen on page 16.

4. The weight to be attached to each of the *Spijkers* criteria will vary according to the activity carried on.
5. If the economic entity can function without significant assets, the maintenance of its identity cannot depend upon the transfer of any such assets.
6. Where the assets are owned and they are required to run the undertaking, the fact that they do not transfer does not preclude a transfer.
7. If maintenance work is carried out by a cleaning firm which is then taken over by the owner of the premises this does not, of itself, point to a transfer.
8. Similarity of the service provided by an old and new service provider, does not, of itself, mean that there has been a transfer.
9. The absence of a contractual link between the transferor and the transferee may be evidence that there has been no transfer, but this is not conclusive. A contractual link is not necessary.
10. Where no employees are transferred, the reason for them not transferring may be relevant.
11. The fact that the work continues uninterrupted and without a change is a normal feature of a transfer of an undertaking. The fact that there is a gap between the finished work by one contractor and the start of the work by the successor has no particular importance.

2.5 DIRECTION IN 2001

After this ruling it seemed that the case law was moving in a consistent direction. However, the period of certainty and consolidation was ended when the ECJ threw the law into confusion with their ruling in the case of *Oy Liikenne Ab* v. *Liskojärvi* (C-172/99) [2001] IRLR 171, ECJ.

This case was referred to the ECJ from Finland. The ruling in this matter unfortunately followed *Suzen* and emphasised the need for a transfer of assets or, where there were no or few assets, the transfer of a significant part of the workforce. This now places the law in a considerable state of doubt as the UK courts had been moving away from *Suzen*; but now the ECJ may have placed new emphasis on *Suzen* being the correct interpretation of the law.

The facts of the case were that the Helsinki Council tendered for the right to run bus routes. The outgoing contractor lost the contract and it was awarded to Oy Liikenne Ab. The outgoing contractor owned 26 buses and dismissed 45 people. The incoming contractor purchased its own buses and re-engaged 33 of the 45 drivers and hired another 18 of its own on less favourable terms and conditions of employment. It therefore took over a majority of the workforce but no assets. It did buy some uniforms from the outgoing contractor, but that was all. The arguments put forward by the incoming contractor to avoid the Directive were as follows:

1. There was no contractual relationship with the outgoing contractor.
2. Bus routes did not amount to an economic entity.
3. The assets of the outgoing contractor were not taken over by the incoming contractor.
4. Drivers were engaged at their own request; the incoming contractor was free to hire who it wanted.
5. Because there is mandatory competitive tendering in the transport sector (EC Directive 92/50), it was undesirable to apply the traditional transfer of undertakings approach because it acted as a disincentive to contractors in the tendering process.

The employees argued that:

1. An absence of a direct contractual relationship may point to a lack of transfer but this is not conclusive.
2. The aim of the Acquired Rights Directive is to protect the interest of workers where there is a change in the ownership of an economic entity.
3. It is not intended to exempt service providers from the obligations that apply to other employers even though there is mandatory competitive tendering in the transport sector. Contractors are expected to take the Acquired Rights Directive into account when putting tenders together.

It was held by the ECJ that despite the majority of the workforce moving over, the lack of transfer of the main assets (buses) led to the conclusion that the entity did not retain its identity and therefore the Directive did not apply. The reasoning here is unclear as many of the quotes appearing in the judgment do not indicate whether they were going back to the reasoning of *Suzen* or if they were following other more recent decisions. In its decision the ECJ took account of *Cheesman*. All the factors identified in *Cheesman* case were present save for one, namely the reason why the employees did not transfer. The ECJ failed to consider the issue of deliberate avoidance or evasion of the Directive. Great weight was placed upon the fact that no buses transferred and little weight was placed upon the fact that the transferee continued with the same activity after the transfer.

We have to wait for a clarification of this case in order to establish whether or not *Suzen* is now the preferred interpretation of the Directive. The Finnish case appears to put great emphasis upon the fact that no assets transferred; the wider approach of the *Spijkers* checklist was not applied. It is difficult to predict whether the failure to transfer assets and staff may once again be seen to be an effective way of avoiding the effects of the Directive and thus its implementing national regulations. There appear to be tensions between the development of jurisprudence in the UK jurisdiction and in the ECJ. It seems that the ruling in *ECM* goes beyond that of the Directive. Could it be said that the decision of *ECM* is now in doubt in the light of the ruling in the ECJ? It may, however, be that *Oy Liikenne* can be distinguished on its facts as applying solely to the transfer of public transport contracts.

2.6 CLARIFICATION ON *ADI*

Since the case of *Oy Liikenne* there has been another Court of Appeal decision on the issue of whether there is an economic entity and in the case of *ADI (UK) Ltd* v. *Willer* [2001] IRLR 542. ADI provided security services at a shopping centre. It terminated the contract and the shopping centre initially stated that it would take over the employment of the nine security officers. Following a dispute with the security officers regarding terms and conditions of employment, the shopping centre then said that it would was no longer prepared not take on any of the officers.

The Court of Appeal (by majority) held that there had been a transfer. The court considered the two following questions:

(a) whether the tribunal was under a duty to consider whether the shopping centre had avoided taking on staff to avoid the effect of the TUPE regulations; and

(b) if so, the effect of that.

With regard to the first issue, there was an obligation on the tribunal to investigate the reason for the shopping centre's failing to take on any of the staff, provided that the issue was raised by one of the parties. With regard to the second issue, it was held that transferees could not escape the effect of TUPE by simply refusing to take on any of the workforce. Therefore if the transferee failed to take on any of the employees to avoid there being a transfer the tribunal had to treat the case as if it had taken on all the staff. This point was unfortunately conceded by the transferee and was therefore not fully argued by the court. However, it is clear from the ruling that the court was applying and reinforcing the decision of *ECM*, if only by a majority decision.

Lord Justice May referred to the fact that 'the concept of transfer is now a judicially constructed fiction derived from the purpose of the Directive and the Regulations to safeguard the rights of employees'. He considered the cases of *Allen* v. *Amalgamated*, *Oy Liikenne* and *Suzen* and decided that a mere provision of the same service at the shopping centre did not support the contention that an economic entity had transferred. 'An economic entity cannot be reduced to an activity entrusted to it.' However, this was a labour-intensive activity. What had to be asked, therefore, was why none of the workforce was transferred. If the reason was to avoid the effects of the TUPE regulations, then the regulations would be deemed to apply. The matter was remitted to tribunal to consider the point. Lord Justice Brown gave a dissenting judgment, arguing that the decision of *ECM* was not supported by ECJ authorities.

If this is the way in which the TUPE regulations are to be interpreted then there is a clear indication that we are moving again in the direction of the purposive approach. However, only time will tell.

2.7 SECOND GENERATION CONTRACTING OUT: RECENT DEVELOPMENTS

Two more cases have dealt with second generation contracting out and back in and both appear to restate the well-founded principles established in previous cases. However, the first case came to a surprising conclusion that the TUPE regulations did not apply to bringing services back in house. The reason for that conclusion is dealt with in the case of *Ministry of Defence* v. *Carvey and others and Rentokil Initial Services Ltd* (EAT, 26 April 2001).

Rentokil were contracted by the Ministry of Defence (MOD) to provide guards for an army site from 1991 to 1999. In 1999 the MOD set up an internal unit for guarding Category A sites and they bought the guarding of the site back in house. Ten employees who were employed by Rentokil were not kept on by them or by the MOD. The employees pursued a claim that they had either:

(a) been made redundant by Rentokil or
(b) been transferred by the MOD under TUPE, in which case they had been unfairly dismissed.

The EAT found that an economic entity cannot be reduced to an activity entrusted to it, so the fact that an activity remains the same does not necessarily indicate the existence of a relevant transfer. The fact that the labour force of a labour intensive entity is not taken on does not necessarily indicate the absence of a relevant transfer – all the circumstances of the case must be taken into account. The EAT found that the tribunal was wrong to have concluded that there had been the transfer of an undertaking. The EAT found that the MOD had established two reasons for failing to take on the staff and they were:

(a) for overriding economic reasons; and
(b) because they wished to employ in-house armed guards.

As the MOD had not attempted to defeat or avoid the operation of the regulations by dismissing staff, the *ECM* case could not be used to 'infer' a transfer.

This case suggests that an overriding economic reason is a bona fide reason for a prospective transferee to refuse to take on an outgoing contractor's workforce. This must (with respect) be wrong as it would mean that any transferee could fairly dismiss employees who were earning a higher rate of pay to avoid the burden of taking on higher paid members of staff. This could be clarified by the Employment Relations Act 1999, s.38, which allows the government to extend the protection of TUPE to employees who would otherwise not be protected by the Directive.

The consultation document that was published in September 2001 (see Appendix 4) also suggested that the regulations should apply to all contracting out situations except in very rare circumstances. It may be that the necessity for guards to be armed and the interests of public security would be one of those exceptions.

The second case that dealt with second generation contracting out at arm's length was *Temco Service Industries SA* v. *Imzilyen and others* (C-51/00) (ECJ, 24 January 2002). Cleaning services were contracted out in the Volkswagen plant in Belgium. The contract was then terminated with one company (which had subcontracted the work to another company) and another company reached agreement with Volkswagen, to which the work passed. The new contractor took on part of the staff of the subcontractor but took on no other tangible or intangible assets. As the staff taken on were an essential part, in terms of their numbers and skill, to the performance of the subcontract, they amounted to an organised grouping of wage-earners who were specifically and permanently assigned to a common task. This might, therefore, in the absence of other factors, amount to an economic entity. However, this did not preclude the right of a worker to remain with the transferor if the employee objected to the transfer of the employment contract or the employment relationship with the transferee. The court reaffirmed some basic principles, which were that:

1. There need not be any contractual link between the outgoing transferor and the transferee. In this case the transferor was one step removed from the contracting process itself.
2. Employees who are dismissed prior to the transfer, but for a reason connected with the transfer, cannot be denied their rights to have their contract maintained by the transferee.
3. In labour-intensive sectors, a group of workers engaged in a joint activity on a permanent basis may constitute an economic entity. Such an entity is therefore capable of maintaining its identity after it has been transferred, where the new employer does not merely pursue the activity in question but also takes over a major part, in terms of the numbers and skills of the employees specially assigned by the predecessor to the task. Therefore an organised grouping of wage-earners who are specifically and permanently assigned to a common task, may, in the absence of other factors, amount to an economic entity.
4. The fact that the transferee was forced to take on staff under the terms of a collective agreement had no bearing upon whether the Directive applied. The transferred activity was an economic entity in its own right.
5. The decisive criteria in establishing whether there is a transfer for the purposes of the Directive is whether the business retains its identity.

CHAPTER 3

Different forms of transfer

3.1 PUBLIC SECTOR TRANSFERS?

The 1977 Acquired Rights Directive did not apply to transfers of a purely administrative function as they were thought not to fall within the definition of an 'economic entity'. It was felt that the Directive would not apply to any public function, whether or not it was operating as an economic function. This notion was challenged in the case of *Dr Sophie Redmond*, which confirmed that the economic activity did not have to be in the nature of a commercial venture for the Directive to apply. This left the door open to extending the definition of the Directive to transfers within the public sector if they were operating an economic activity that was more than a merely administrative activity. Since this case, the Directive has been interpreted narrowly to exclude only the purely administrative functions of government departments.

Henke v. *Gemeinde Schierke* (C-298/94) [1996] IRLR 701, ECJ involved a government organisation where administrative tasks were transferred from one local government body to another; in the process, Mrs Henke lost her job. It was held by the ECJ that was not a transfer because it involved an administrative function and not an economic activity. This decision is irreconcilable with previous cases such as *Dr Sophie Redmond*, and is out of line with the way in which the law was previously heading. The next two cases sought to define the words 'administrative function' narrowly and to give a wide interpretation to the words 'economic entity' and 'activity' in line with the decision of *Dr Sophie Redmond*.

The facts of *Mayeur* v. *Association Promotion de l'Information Messine (APIM)* (C-175/99) [2000] IRLR 783, ECJ were that M was employed by a non-profit-making association responsible for the publication of a magazine promoting the city of Metz. In 1987 APIM was dissolved and the activities were taken over by the city of Metz itself and M was dismissed. Under French law, the Directive did not apply to transfers to public bodies (as in the case of *Henke*). It was held by the ECJ that the facts of *Mayeur* were that the transfer of an economic activity from a legal person governed by public law in principle fell under the Directive. The Directive applied to the transfer of *any* stable economic entity, being defined as 'an organised grouping of persons and assets facilitating the exercise of an economic activity that pursues a specific objective'. *Henke* did not apply in this situation as it turned on its own narrow facts, those being this was a transfer of administrative function involving the exercise of a public authority.

In *Mayeur* there was a transfer of an economic entity between two distinct bodies: the distinct economic entity was the publicity and information activities carried on by APIM which were transferred to Metz. The entity had also retained its identity after the transfer, which was an essential part of the test, as it was found that Metz had taken it over in its entirety and pursued the activity of APIM in continuing to produce and distribute the magazine.

It was also confirmed in this case that an entity could not be reduced to an activity entrusted to it. Other factors such as its workforce, its managerial staff, the way in which its work was organised, its operating methods or the operational resources available contributed to its identity. The Directive, therefore, applied.

The third case of *Collino* v. *Telecom Italia SpA* [2000] IRLR 788, ECJ then followed the *Mayeur* lead. It was found that the Directive applied to a public body transferring a telephone service for value to a wholly state-owned private company. The case also confirmed that the Directive would apply only to those employees who would have been protected under national law. The case involved two employees who had transferred to Telecom Italia. They sought the right to enjoy salary increases based on their length of service both before and after the transfer. Their severance packages were less than they would have received had they been based on their entire unbroken service with the transferor and the transferee.

The court held that the Directive applied to all transactions unless the activity in question involved the exercise of a public authority and reorganisation of the structures of public administration or the transfer of administrative functions between public administration authorities, as in the case of *Henke*. The case also confirmed that the Directive only applied to 'persons who are protected in the members states concerned as workers under National Labour Law'.

The new guidance on public sector transfers

A Statement of Practice was issued by the government to clarify the implications of the TUPE regulations when staff transferred from the public to private sector under public private partnership (PPP) deals. The Statement took effect from January 2000 and stated that:

1. The TUPE regulations will apply to all PPP deals unless there are genuine, exceptional reasons for them not to do so.
2. The regulations should be followed even in circumstances where they did not apply in strict legal terms.
3. Appropriate arrangements should be made to protect occupational pensions, redundancy and severance terms of staff in transfer situations.

The Statement applied directly to central government departments and agencies under the NHS. Public sector organisations were also expected to follow the principles set out.

The revised EC Business Transfers Directive as amended by the Council Directive No. 2001/23/EC had to be implemented by member states by 17 July 2001 (see Appendix 1). In this amendment there is an expanded definition of the scope of the Directive. The new art. 1(1) (c) provides that

> this Directive shall apply to Public and Private Undertakings engaging in economic activities whether or not they are operating for a gain. An administrative re-organisation of Public Administrative Authorities, or the transfer of administrative functions between Public Administrative Authorities, is not a transfer within the meaning of this Directive.

This provision gives effect to the ECJ's interpretation of the Directive in *Henke* and is in line with the reasoning adopted in the cases of *Collino* and *Mayeur*. The UK's government policy is that employees in the public sector should be treated no less favourably than private sector employees when they are part of an organised grouping of resources transferred between public sector employers. This issue is to be addressed by the application of the government's Statement above and with regards to the Employment Relations Act 1999, s.38, which effectively extends the TUPE regulations 1981 to situations which would otherwise fall outside the scope of the Directive.

3.2 OTHER FORMS OF RELEVANT TRANSFER

Part of an undertaking

The TUPE regulations also apply when part of an undertaking is transferred 'as a going concern'. They will clearly apply to transfers that are more than a mere transfer of assets. What has to be considered is whether:

(a)   the part a self-contained or severable part;
(b)   it is geographically separate; or
(c)   it is a distinct and severable activity.

In *GD Ault (Isle of Wight) Ltd* v. *Gregory* (1967) 3 KIR 590, 2 ITR 30, Div Ct, the transferor company was a property developer on the Isle of Wight and in Reading. It sold off the Isle of Wight branch, including stock, plant equipment and goodwill. It was held that this was an undertaking that was transferred as a going concern. In *Secretary of State for Employment* v. *Spence* [1986] 3 All ER 616 it was held that it was not essential that a workforce existed for an undertaking to be capable of being transferred as a going concern.

Transfers between subsidiaries

The TUPE regulations can apply to transfers between subsidiaries, as was seen in the case of *Allen* v. *Amalgamated Construction Co. Ltd* [2000] IRLR 119, ECJ. Amalgamated Construction Company (AC) and AM Mining (AM) were wholly owned subsidiaries of AMCO Corporation (AMCO). Both AM and AC were distinct legal entities but with the same management, administrative assistants and support within the parent company. AC carried out driveage work at sites and AM carried out work ancillary to driveage. AC had more favourable terms and conditions of employment.

AC tendered for work on the understanding that the work would be subcontracted out to AM, where labour costs were lower. AC dismissed a number of staff informing them that they could be taken on after a break of a weekend by AM. The re-engagement did not coincide with the beginning or end of any contracts. There was no transfer of assets. Upon re-engagement the employees' terms and conditions were better than those at AM but worse than those at AC. The employees claimed that they were entitled to the original terms and conditions of AC. The case was referred to the ECJ by the Leeds Employment Tribunal.

It was held by the ECJ that:

1. The Directive can apply whether the change in the natural or legal person and it can also apply to a transfer between two subsidiary companies in the same group. The fact that the companies are under the same ownership makes no difference.
2. The criterion is whether the undertaking retains its identity. The undertaking must be a stable economic entity and its activity not limited to performing one specific contract. The entity must be an organised grouping of persons and assets facilitating the exercise of an economic activity which pursues a specific objective.
3. A group of workers engaged in a joint activity could constitute an economic entity capable of maintaining its identity where a new employer took over the activity and employees. It was not of decisive importance that there was no transfer of assets.
4. It was not held to be of importance that the dismissal of employees was not contemporaneous with the subcontracting out of the work. It was found that the dismissal and re-engagement of employees was clearly connected with the subcontracting and therefore the TUPE regulations applied.

It is clear from this case that subcontracting between subsidiaries will be found to be within the regulations even where dismissals may be remote from the time of the transfer. There are therefore now very few ways of avoiding a relevant transfer that will attract the TUPE provisions.

Sale or some other disposition or operation of law

A transfer can be effected by sale or otherwise irrespective of whether it is a voluntary act by act of party or involuntary by operation of law, of whether the transaction is governed by English law or not, or of whether it is effected by one transaction or a series or transactions. It can also occur even when no property is transferred. The concept of a legal transfer requires no more than consent between the transferor and the transferee, even if the transfer results from a unilateral declaration or an act of a third party and even if no agreement is concluded between the transferor and the transferee.

Transfer by sale of shares

The only certain way to avoid the TUPE regulations is to arrange the transfer as a sale or purchase of shares. The courts are reluctant to lift the corporate veil unless there is evidence to show that it is being used as a device to avoid TUPE. This was the case in *Brookes* v. *Borough Care Services* [1998] IRLR 636, [1998] ICR 1198, EAT. The transfer was deliberately rearranged as a sale of shares after the case of *Wilson* v. *St Helens* (see below) as the transferee wished to impose post-transfer contractual changes on the employees' contracts of employment. The courts would not lift the corporate veil and compromise the principle that share transfers were excluded from both the Directive and the TUPE regulations. The regulations can therefore effectively be avoided by the company transferring its shares.

Changes in the employer

It has been held that there need be no legal change of ownership of the business in order for there to be a transfer – a change in employer alone can amount to a transfer. This was found in the case of *Landsorganisationen i Danmark* v. *Ny Molle Kro* (C-287/86) [1989] IRLR 37, [1989] ICR 330, ECJ, where the ECJ stressed that the important factor in applying the Directive was not whether there was an actual change in the ownership of the business, but rather whether there was any change in the person who assumed the capacity of the employer. Therefore the Directive applied to circumstances in which a managing lessee acquired the capacity of an employer under the terms of a lease. In *Landsorganisationen* the lease in question was the lease of a tavern, which was leased from H to L. L concluded an agreement with the Association of Hotel Employees whereby a collective agreement was entered into for minimum wages to be paid to the hotel staff. There was a subsequent breach of the lease and it reverted back to H.

After the reversion, a waitress called Mrs Hansen sued for wages owed to her and claimed that she was paid less than was owing to her under the collective agreement. The issue was whether there had been a relevant transfer of the lease when it reverted back to H after the breach of the lease. In arguments it was put forward that the Directive speaks of transfer to another employer rather than to another owner. The ECJ held that:

1. The purpose of the Acquired Rights Directive was to safeguard the rights of workers in the event of a change in the identity of the employer, by allowing them to remain in the employment of the new employer on the same conditions as those that had been agreed with the employees and the transferor.

2. The Directive applies whenever there is a change in the natural or legal person responsible for the running of the business, who enters into contractual obligations as an employer, regardless of whether the ownership of the undertaking has been transferred. The employees of an undertaking where the employer is changed without the transfer of ownership need the same protection as those in the employment of an undertaking which is sold.

3. Therefore, in the current case, the managing lessee acquired the capacity of employer under the terms of the lease. The transfer of the lease constituted a transfer of an undertaking to another employer as a result of a legal transfer under art. 1(1). When the owner of the lease took back the running of the business, this amounted to a transfer as the lessee lost the capacity of employer, which transferred to the lessor.

It is clear under TUPE reg. 3(2) that a transfer can be effected by 'sale or other disposition or by operation of law'. The words 'some other disposition' cover all other forms of transfer, which include gifts and reversions of business leases, the termination and grants of franchises, licences and concessions. The case below, heard after the decision of *Ny Molle Kro*, shows the extent to which the courts are prepared to interpret the words or 'or other disposition' to find that there has been a relevant transfer in order to protect employees' rights after the sale or transfer of a business.

Lease-purchase agreements

Berg and Busschers v. *Besselsen* (C-144, 145/87) [1989] IRLR 447, [1990] ICR 396, ECJ involved the transfer of a bar disco. The business was owned by Besselsen but the operation of the company was taken over by Summerland under a lease-purchase agreement, which did not transfer the business immediately. The employees started working for Summerland before the business transferred. The business did not transfer legally to Summerland and after nine months the business reverted to Besselsen. The employees sued both Besselsen and Summerland for arrears of wages owed when Summerland was the employer. The decision of *Ny Molle Kro* was followed. The Directive applied even when there had been a simple change in the employer and not a change in legal ownership. When the lease-purchase agreement was entered into the responsibility for the payment of wages passed to Summerland, along with the general management responsibilities. That responsibility reverted to

41

Besselsen when the lease-purchase agreement was set aside. Besselsen was therefore responsible for all the arrears of wages. The ECJ held that:

1. The transfer of an undertaking entails an automatic transfer from the transferor to the transferee of the employer's obligations arising from the contract of employment or from an employment relationship.
2. The transferor is released from its obligations as an employer solely by reason of the transfer and this legal consequence is not conditional upon the consent of the employees concerned and cannot be prevented by their objection to it.
3. The Directive is intended to safeguard the rights of workers in the event of a change of employer, making it possible for them to continue to work for the transferee under the same conditions as those agreed with the transferor. The relationship does not continue when the employee does not wish to remain in the transferee's employment.
4. The automatic transfer of obligations in the Directive safeguards existing employment relationships which are part of the economic entity transferred. Any national rule regarding the transfer of a debt that provides for the fact that a debt may only be transferred with the creditor's consent is overruled by the Directive. The debt therefore, is passed back to Besselsen under the terms of the Directive.

It is clear, therefore, that when management responsibilities are transferred, there will in all possibility be a relevant transfer. Both transferor and transferee need to be aware of their responsibilities to employees who transfer, otherwise they may face litigation in respect of contractual changes, unfair dismissal, Wages Act claims, etc. Those advising in connection with business reorganisations or restructuring need to be fully aware of the likelihood of such transfers in order to advise the new management structures of their liabilities.

The transfer of a subsidy

In *Dr Sophie Redmond Stichting* v. *Bartol* C-29/91 [1992] IRLR 366 it was held that the transfer of a subsidy from one foundation engaged in assisting drug addicts to another amounted to a relevant transfer.

The transfer of a service

In *Kenny* v. *South Manchester College* [1993] IRLR 265 the transfer of a prison education service from a local education authority to South Manchester College without a transfer of assets, clients, customers or employees was held to amount to a relevant transfer.

Transfer by operation of law

In *Charlton* v. *Charlton Thermosystems (Romsey) Ltd* [1995] IRLR 79, [1995] ICR 56 there was a transfer of undertaking when the director and sole shareholders of a company continued trading for several weeks after it was struck off the Register of Companies for failing to submit final accounts. The employees were kept on during the period and when they were finally dismissed the directors became personally liable to the employees for wages owed. The EAT found that the business retained its identity in the hands of the former directors of the dissolved company.

Gifts

The gift of a business from one person to another can be a relevant transfer as seen in the case of *Brooks* v. *The Grays Co-operative Society Ltd* [1967] ITR 345.

Temporary management

It was held in the case of *Vaux Breweries Ltd* v. *Tutty and others* (EAT 33/95) that taking over by a brewery of an insolvent social club for two months until it was sold was a relevant transfer.

Subcontracting

In the case of *Farmer* v. *Danzas (UK) Ltd* (EAT 858/93) there was a relevant transfer when the owner of a subcontracting company and his staff were taken over as employees by the subcontracting company.

Transfer of a dealership

The transfer of a dealership from one motor company to another was held to be a relevant transfer in the case of *Merckx and another* v. *Ford Motor Company Belgium SA* (C-171, 172/94) [1996] IRLR 467, ECJ.

Licences

When an informal licence was granted to a company to use machinery in order to complete a contracted out industrial process, a relevant transfer took place. This was seen in the case of *CWW Logistics* v. *Ronald and Digital Equipment (Scotland) Ltd* (EAT 774/98).

The label attached to the transaction by the parties

This was considered to be of importance in the case of *McLeod* v. *Phoenix Taxies & Rainbow Taxies* (EAT, 22 April 2002). The facts of this case were that Phoenix Taxies sold its business to Rainbow Taxies and the employment tribunal found that there was no transfer, as:

- no assets had transferred;
- no staff had transferred;
- no premises had transferred;
- the only thing that transferred was the use of the business name and the telephone number.

The business also ceased to retain its identity after the sale. After considering *Spijkers* it was held that there was no transfer. There was an appeal to the EAT and it was held that insufficient weight was given to the label in the agreement that it was a sale of a business. The EAT substituted a finding that a transfer had occurred to which the TUPE regulations applied. It may be that the label attached by the parties may now be of weight in deciding whether a relevant transfer has occurred.

Other transfers

Other transfers by law that can amount to relevant transfers under the TUPE regulations include the automatic succession of property from a deceased sole trader to a personal representative. Transfers that result from court orders, for example the appointment of a trustee in bankruptcy, could also amount to a transfer by operation of law.

3.3 INSOLVENCY

Regulation 4, as amended by the Transfer of Undertakings (Protection of Employment) (Amendment) Regulations 1987 (SI 1987/442) contains special rules about hiving down in order to preserve the freedom of a liquidator, receiver or administrator. The hiving down scheme was introduced to allow the liquidator, receiver or administrator to form a wholly owned subsidiary of the company and transfer ownership of that company or the salvageable part of the company to a purchaser. The employees are retained in the parent company and are hired out to the subsidiary company to enable it to maintain the business as a going concern without actually employing anyone. The subsidiary's business or the subsidiary itself can then be offered for sale as a clean package free from the claims of the workforce but allowing the purchaser to pick and choose any employees that it may wish to employ. This prevents claims being made by employees against the purchaser of a business, which might deter any rescuers of the business or would make the package an unattractive prospect.

Hiving down is specifically preserved by the TUPE regulations, which state that a transfer under these circumstances is not held to be as 'immediately before a relevant transfer'. The immediate transfer is kept in suspense as long as the subsidiary company remains a wholly owned subsidiary. The provisions apply to all receiverships but only to creditors' voluntary winding up. Although hiving down has the effect of depriving the workforce of rights provided under TUPE to protect employee status and contractual statutory rights, it is seen to be a compromise for the greater good, as without this provision it would be likely that a business would not be purchased and an opportunity of saving jobs would thus be missed. At the very least the provisions allow the possibility of saving some jobs and the state, therefore, assumes responsibility (by way of paying benefits) for those who are not taken on. The protection given to hiving down was challenged in the famous case of *Litster* v. *Forth Dry Dock and Engineering Company Ltd* [1989] 1 All ER 1134, [1989] IRLR 161. In this case a company had gone into receivership and the receivers successfully negotiated a sale and a newly formed company called Forth Estuary Engineering Limited (the transferee) was incorporated with the objective of taking over the business of the company in receivership. One hour before the sale the receivers dismissed the entire workforce at the request of the transferee. Forty-eight hours later some of the employees were recruited by the transferee on less attractive terms and conditions. The Lords held that all employees were dismissed solely or principally because of the relevant transfer, and that they therefore had to be regarded as being employed 'immediately before the transfer' for the purposes of reg. 5(3). This was a direct challenge to the practices that had been developed within the TUPE regulations. In this case the receivers were able to avail themselves of the defence of an ETO under reg. 8(2). However, this case has left insolvency practitioners exposed and facing the prospect of claims for unfair dismissal.

In the case of *Thompson* v. *SCS Consulting Ltd and others* (EAT, 3 September 2001) it was held that employees who were dismissed 11 hours before the insolvent business was transferred by receivers, were dismissed because they were not required for the operation of the business. The business was not economically viable and therefore it could not continue with its current workforce. It was held that the reason for the dismissal amounted to an ETO and therefore that the dismissal was not automatically unfair.

Article 5 of the new Council Directive 2001/23/EC provides that arts. 3 (relating to the transfer of employees' rights and obligations arising from an employment relationship) and 4 (providing that the transfer shall not constitute grounds for dismissal) shall not apply where bankruptcy or insolvency proceedings are being pursued with a view to the liquidation of assets. The liquidation must be carried out by a 'competent public authority'.

Article 5 provides that the transferor's debts relating to the termination of the employees' contracts of employment shall not pass to the transferee, provided there is adequate protection for employees in the event of insolvency, or if any alterations are agreed by the employee representatives, the transferee and the transferor (or the person exercising the function of the transferor). The alterations that are agreed must be reached with a view to the survival of the business. It is clear that these provisions apply only to the rights afforded to employees under arts. 3 and 4. They do not absolve the insolvency practitioner from the duty to inform and consult under art. 7.

As penalties are now levied for failure to inform and consult, all insolvency practitioners are advised to take this obligation seriously, as failure to do so may result in complaints being submitted to the employment tribunal for compensation of up to 13 weeks' gross pay per employee (see Chapter 4).

It is clear from art. 5(4) of the Directive that a dim view will be taken of any misuse of insolvency proceedings commenced to deprive employees of their rights under the Directive. Article 5(4) states that 'Member States shall take appropriate measures with a view to preventing misuse of insolvency proceedings in such a way as to deprive employees of the rights provided for in this Directive'.

It has now been accepted that the hiving down provisions may no longer serve any useful purpose. In the light of the new provisions contained in the Directive, the public consultation document (see Appendix 4) confirms at para. 33 that the government believes that in the light of the recent case law the existing provisions in reg. 4 relating to hiving down no longer serve any useful purpose and the provisions will therefore be removed.

The following cases show a further development of the courts' willingness to adopt a purposive approach in the definition of what amounts to a relevant transfer, where the insolvency of a company leaves employees uncompensated and without a remedy.

Kerry Foods v. *Creber* [2000] IRLR 10, EAT was a case concerning a sausage making factory that fell into financial difficulties. Receivers were appointed on 24 January 1995, a Friday. Non-essential staff were sacked on Monday 27 January 1995 and all other staff were then dismissed on 31 January 1995. Kerry Foods then purchased the brand name and goodwill. No staff were taken on but Kerry Foods continued to manufacture sausages at a different location. Any remaining staff were sacked on the day of the purchase. Staff brought claims for unfair dismissal against the purchasers of the business. It was held that there was a relevant transfer even though no employees transferred and the company did not continue to manufacture sausages at the former employees' factory. The findings in *ECM* were therefore approved.

In *In re Maxwell Fleet and Facilities Management Ltd (in administration)* [2000] IRLR 368 the High Court determined that where a receiver, administrator or liquidator of a company transfers the undertaking to a third party purchaser, having first hived down the assets and business to a subsidiary company which then dismissed the employees before transferring on to a purchaser, this series of transactions will be caught by the TUPE regulations so that the liability under the contact of employment will pass to the ultimate transferee. In this case the High Court was able to defeat a device set up to evade the regulations by carrying out the transfer through an intermediary. This device was adopted to transfer the business stripped of the existing liability to the employees. This was clearly a device to avoid TUPE and the court adopted a purposive approach introduced by the case of *Litster* (see above, p.7) to look behind the labyrinth of structures that had been set up solely for the purposes of avoiding the TUPE provisions.

As the legal debate shows, there is no definite and identifiable definition of the terms 'relevant transfer' and 'undertaking'. This makes it difficult to advise transferors, transferees or employees as to their legal rights and obligations with certainty. In many cases the facts may be clear, but where there is doubt it would be prudent to assume that the TUPE regulations apply in order to avoid costly and time-consuming legal challenges in the employment tribunals.

3.4   ADVICE AT THE PRE-TRANSFER STAGE

If instructed at the pre-transfer stage, advice must be given on the likelihood of the TUPE regulations applying and the effect that this may have on the cost of the venture and the likely exposure to the risk of claims being made by employees. In respect of all business transfers, a risk assessment must be carried out of whether the TUPE regulations apply in order for the parties to make provision for the financial and legal costs of complying with the provisions and to fulfil their obligations to inform and consult. The advice to be given at an early stage to all parties may include the following matters.

Advice to the transferor

Before a transfer takes place and at negotiation stage, the practical aspects of TUPE must be taken into consideration. Advice must be given on the type of transfer to adopt and the effect that the transfer may have upon the rights of employees who transfer and those (if any) who do not. The following aspects should be considered when advising the transferor.

The TUPE regulations will apply to preserve the rights of employees in most dispositions. These will include any of the following transactions:

- sales, mergers and acquisitions;
- transfers of whole or part of an organisation;
- franchises, licences, concessions and grants;
- transfers of leases;
- transfers of subsidies;
- transfers between subsidiaries;
- contracting out;
- leases and leasebacks;
- insolvency;

- dissolution of the corporate structure;
- changes in the management structure.

When advising on the disposition of a business or business premises using any of these methods, it is important to ask whether there are any employees of the business and what will happen to those employees on the disposition. Often the rights of employees are overlooked when it is believed that the TUPE regulations do not apply to the transfer. As can be seen from the above case law, it is difficult to be certain that they will not apply; it is therefore prudent to advise on the premise that they will. Even if the transfer appears to be merely a disposition of a property used for business purposes, a caretaker or cleaning and security staff employed to service the building may have the protection of the regulations by being assigned to the business or part transferred.

If a client requests guidance on methods of avoiding TUPE, advice must be given that the courts will now look to the intentions of the parties and the reason why none of the employees was taken on, as in the case of *ADI* (see section 2.6). When a transferor is asked for advice on the dismissal of staff, clear advice must be given that tribunals will conduct an investigation into the reasons for the dismissals, and that if they are for a reason connected with the transfer, the dismissals may be found to be automatically unfair (unless there is a defence of an ETO – see Chapter 6).

The only way to avoid TUPE is to effect a disposition by sale of shares; but caution needs to be advised as the courts have been known to pierce the corporate veil where it is used as a device to avoid the regulations. The courts now look at the intentions of the parties, and if the transaction is seen as a device invoked in order to avoid the effects of the regulations, the court may find that there has been a relevant transfer.

The TUPE regulations do not provide protection to independent contractors, consultants and casual workers as they adopt the narrower definition of employee. However, one must view with suspicion those who work on long-term assignments via employment agencies, as in the case of *Motorola Limited* v. *Davidson and Melville Craig Group Limited* [2001] IRLR 4, EAT, or those who are paid as independent contractors but who are in substance and form employees. They may held to be employees, as seen in the case of *Ready Mixed Concrete* (see 2.1).

It has been clarified in case law that the TUPE regulations and the Directive only protect those who have employment law rights and interests under domestic law. They do not provide employees with additional rights; thus they do not give those who have been employed for less than one year the right to claim for unfair dismissal. Employees with less than one year's service will still have claims for breach of contract and their statutory rights. Only those with one or more years' service have a right to claim for unfair dismissal. There is no claim in equity for remedies such as injunctions or specific performance. When advising as to the risk of litigation, all potential liabilities must be taken into account.

If a relevant transfer is likely to take place, the best way forward is to assume that whatever disposition or restructure is proposed, TUPE will apply. Working on that assumption, both the transferor and the transferee will need to follow the requirements to inform and consult employees as set out in the next section. Plenty of time should be allowed for this to take place.

If the transferor is to dismiss anyone and the dismissal could be deemed to be connected with the transfer, then it would be advisable to cover the dismissal with a compromise agreement. This would prevent the employee from lodging any claims in the employment tribunal for unfair dismissal, although a termination by way of a compromise agreement would cost more to the transferor as (to be effective) independent legal advice must be provided. It is likely that, when adopting a compromise agreement, an ex gratia payment may have to be made. However, it would protect the value of the transferor's business in the process of negotiations for sale and it would protect the interests of the transferee after the sale. Any compromise agreements negotiated with employees in the weeks leading up to a sale or transfer of the business should be attached to any sale agreement (but see Chapter 6, p.127 regarding the effectiveness of compromise agreements).

If a transfer or sale of a business is being considered, it would be prudent to place an embargo upon all contractual changes to employee contracts. All dismissals should be delayed, except for those that are clearly not connected with the transfer, for example, those for misconduct, retirement and for ill health (but see the provision on pensions in Chapter 7). If any dismissal takes place reasonably proximate to the transfer and the employee lodges a claim for unfair dismissal on the grounds of the transfer, the dismissal may be found to be for a reason connected with the transfer and therefore be deemed automatically unfair.

When contemplating a sale or transfer of a business, the transferor should, at the earliest possible opportunity, create a schedule of all employees who may have the protection of the TUPE regulations and those who do not. It should be assumed that all the employees on both lists will transfer across with the business. The transferor should produce these lists at initial talks with the transferee in order for both parties to identify:

(a) who will transfer;
(b) who will remain with the transferor (if anyone);
(c) the cost implications of any employment liabilities to the value of the business;
(d) the contractual terms (express, implied and incorporated) that apply to each employee.

Advice to the transferee

When taking initial instructions from a purchaser or transferee of a business it must first be established whether the TUPE regulations will apply to the transaction. In order to provide the best possible advice on this pivotal matter, the following issues should be placed before the client in order to establish, on the particular facts of the case, whether a relevant transfer is likely to take place. Those issues are as follows:

1. Is the transfer of a stable economic entity? The identity of the entity arises from the structure of the workforce, the way the work is organised and the operating methods and resources.
2. Is there a relevant transfer of that entity?
3. The *Spijkers* checklist (see p.16) emphasises the fact that even if no assets or staff are transferred, this will not necessarily be decisive of whether or not a relevant transfer has taken place. All the criteria must be considered.
4. If no employees are transferred, the reason for them not transferring may be relevant.
5. A gap between the transferor closing the business and the transferee opening the new business may be of no particular importance.

It is safest to assume that TUPE regulations will apply to the transaction in order for all the correct and fair procedures to be followed. It is always important to stress to the transferee that any elaborate device set up to avoid the regulations applying to the transaction will be closely scrutinised by the courts. If they come to the view that the transaction is put in place with the intention of avoiding the regulations, it will be set aside, as seen in the case of *Maxwell Fleet* (see p.47). The best and safest advice to give any transferee is to presume the TUPE regulations apply. If they are presumed to apply, the duty to inform and consult should be followed (see Chapter 2) and employees will transfer from the transferor to the transferee in accordance with the provisions of reg. 5 (see Chapter 5).

When taking instructions from a prospective purchaser or transferee of a business, it is essential to advise the transferee to obtain the following before confirming the purchase:

(a) a complete list of all employees employed at or near the date of the transfer;

(b) details of all employees' employment history, including age, length of service, salary, job description;

(c) details of all employees dismissed before or reasonably proximate to, the transfer and the reason for the dismissal and copies of any compromise agreements;

(d) details of all collective agreements that exist in the workplace;

(e) details of all contractual rights of employees, including express, implied and incorporated terms together with a copy of the staff handbook and any other non-contractual documents that may apply in the workplace;

(f) details of any contract workers on site, working in security, cleaning or catering functions that may be assigned to the part transferred and details of their length of service as they may be deemed to be employees; and

(g) details of all financial benefits that apply in the workplace, including private health insurance (PHI) schemes, pension schemes and all other employee benefits.

An examination of all of the above documents will help the transferee decide whether the business is a viable prospect. It is only after all of the above information has been obtained that the transferee can establish what employment-related indemnities need to be obtained from the transferor and whether the employees can carry out the expectations of the transferee in respect of the future plans of the business.

The transferee should also be advised to visit the workplace in order to see the operation in action and to talk to the staff. Much can be discovered by talking to those who are actually working in the business. It is often only by talking to staff that seemingly irrelevant issues can be discovered. For example, issues relating to custom and practice, such as Christmas shopping days and bonuses, may not be disclosed by the transferor as they may be deemed to be irrelevancies. Although they may not be entrenched in written terms and conditions they will still be deemed by the employees to be a contractual entitlement. Failure to be aware of these terms may cause considerable employee unrest, poor industrial relations and considerable cost to the business in terms of working hours lost and perhaps claims for breach of contract and constructive unfair dismissal. There is no substitute for direct contact with the workforce who are due to transfer as this will help the transferee to understand their expectations and motivations.

Advice to the employee

Since it is likely that most sales, transfers and reorganisations will be caught by TUPE, advice must be given at an early stage of the employees' right to receive information and to consult if measures are to be taken by the transferor or the transferee. Failure to inform or consult individually or collectively could result in the employee being entitled to claim compensation in the employment tribunal (see Chapter 4).

Aside from the rights to be informed and consulted, all employees have a right to be protected from any contractual changes imposed as a direct result of the transfer. Any dismissals will be automatically unfair unless the employer can set up the defence of an ETO (see Chapter 6).

All employees will transfer to the transferee under the regulations with all of their contractual and statutory rights intact. They should, therefore, be advised that any attempt by either the transferor or the transferee to change contractual terms for a reason connected with the transferor will be unenforceable, and if either attempts to dismiss the employees, the dismissal will be automatically unfair. All compromise agreements that are offered to employees under such circumstances should be looked at carefully to ensure that the employee is being provided with adequate protection or sufficient compensation in the light of these legal protections (but see Chapter 6 on compromise agreements).

CHAPTER 4

Duty to inform and consult

4.1 BACKGROUND TO TUPE

Long before the transfer of an undertaking takes place, there is a duty upon both the transferor and transferee to consult with employees. Originally the TUPE regulations obliged an employer to consult with representatives of an independent trade union recognised by it for the purposes of collective bargaining. If, therefore, an employer did not recognise an independent trade union (or did not recognise an independent trade union for collective bargaining purposes), the obligation was unenforceable. This duty was therefore found to be contrary to art. 6 of the Acquired Rights Directive 77/187/EEC. The case of *EC Commission* v. *UK* (C-382/92) [1994] IRLR 392 held that the provisions in the TUPE regulations did not properly implement the Directive as they only required that consultation took place where an employer recognised a trade union, whereas the Directive referred to workers or their representatives.

As a result of the above case, the Collective Redundancies and Transfer of Undertakings (Protection of Employment) (Amendment) Regulations 1995 (the 1995 regulations) extended the duty to inform and consult where there was no recognised trade union. There was again serious criticism of this amendment as it allowed the employer to choose whether to consult with the recognised trade union or with employee representatives who had been appointed specifically for that purpose. As a result of these criticisms the Collective Redundancies and Transfer of Undertakings (Protection of Employment) (Amendment) Regulations 1999 (the 1999 regulations) removed the option given to employers to choose between the trade union representatives and the employee representatives if the employer recognised a trade union. The 1999 regulations also contained specific requirements to be followed when electing employee representatives. Directive 2001/23/EC, which amended the Acquired Rights Directive, clearly stated at art. 7(6) that:

> Member states shall provide that, where there are no representatives of the employees in an undertaking or business through no fault of their own, the employees concerned must be informed in advance of

> - The date or proposed date of the transfer
> - The reason for the transfer
> - The legal, economic and social implications of the transfer for the employees
> - Any measures envisaged in relation to the employees.

This confirms that where there are no employee representatives, employees must be informed individually, thus increasing the burden upon the employer to inform and consult all those employees affected by the transfer, even where there are no representatives.

As can be seen, UK domestic law has again been slow to bring about full compliance with the Directive with the result that amendments to legislation have begrudgingly moved the UK into line with European law. It is clear that the notion of worker democracy has been extended by the Transnational Information and Consultation of Employees Regulations 1999 which came into force on 15 January 2000. These regulations place an obligation upon employers of undertakings with at least 1,000 employees within the member states and at least 150 employees in each of at least two member states to inform and consult. It is clear that these regulations will apply to transfers of undertakings (or contemplation of transfers) of multinational companies. These regulations also contain heavy penalties for those who fail to comply with their provisions.

The public consultation document at para. 20 (see Appendix 4) confirms that the government intends to place an obligation upon the transferor in a prospective transfer to give to the transferee *written notification* of all rights and obligations in relation to employees who are to be transferred. It is further stated that if any of the rights and obligations in question change between the time of the notification by the transferor and the completion of the transfer, the transferor is required to give the transferee written notification of the change.

The types of notification that are required may be given in more than one instalment, but each instalment must be given:

(a) in good time before completion of the transfer; or

(b) if special circumstances make this not reasonably practicable, as soon as is reasonably practicable and in any case no later than the completion of the transfer.

The notion of industrial democracy seems set to become a feature of the everyday employment law rights of those employees caught up in a transfer. The right to information and consultation will be deemed to be an employee's right.

There is also a new Directive 2002/14/EC (see Appendix 2) establishing a general framework for informing and consulting employees in the European Community. This Directive must be implemented by 2005 in the UK where there are over 150 employees. It is expected that by 2008 it will apply to all businesses that employ more than 50 employees. The Directive will give employees the right to be:

- informed about the business situation;
- informed and consulted about employment prospects (particularly where there is a threat to employment;
- informed and consulted about decisions likely to lead to substantial changes in work, organisation or contractual relations (including redundancies and transfers).

It will be expected that information and consultation must take place at an appropriate time and with the relevant management consultation with trade unions and appropriate representatives. Employers will be entitled to withhold information or disclosure which would seriously harm the company or be prejudicial to it.

We have also seen the notion of statutory recognition for trade unions provided under the Employment Relations Act 1999. The duty to inform and consult trade unions and employee representatives is seen as a vital part of the process of transferring a business, not an option.

4.2 DUTY TO INFORM

The obligation to provide information ultimately falls upon both the transferor and transferee. TUPE reg. 10(2) sets out what information must be disclosed by employers to the appropriate representatives to enable consultations to take place. The information that is required must include:

(a) the fact that the transfer is to take place;

(b)   approximately when it is to take place;
(c)   the reason for the transfer;
(d)   the legal, economic and social implications of the transfer for affected employees (this definition has no interpretative assistance and is a straight lift from the Directive itself);
(e)   the measures that the employer envisages it will take in relation to affected employees in connection with the transfer;
(f)   if the employer is the transferor, the measures that the transferee envisages that it will take, in connection with the transfer, in relation to those employees who become employees of the transferee after the transfer. If no measures are due to be taken after the transfer, confirmation of that fact.

Where the employer is the transferor, it must tell the employees whether the transferee intends to take measures in relation to any employees in connection with the transfer, or if it does not intend to take any measures it must tell the transferor that it does not envisage changes or detail the changes that are envisaged. This information must be provided by the transferee in sufficient time to enable the transferor to perform the duties contained in reg. 10(2). Under reg. 10(3) this information must be provided by the transferee in time to enable the transferor to perform the duties contained in reg. 10(3). This means that the transferee must supply this information to the transferor in a form that will allow compliance with the statutory obligations, i.e. not under commercial confidence (*Institution of Professional Civil Servants* v. *The Secretary of State for Defence* [1987] IRLR 373, [1987] 3 CMLR 35).

The transferor must pass on this information to the appropriate representatives and the recognised trade unions in respect of those employees. It is stated in the TUPE regulations that this information must be delivered or sent by post. The information should therefore be sent by recorded delivery or delivered to *all* appropriate representatives at an address provided by the transferor and in the case of recognised trade unions sent to union headquarters (reg. 10(4)).

Under the public consultation document an obligation will shortly be placed upon the employer transferor to provide to the transferee written notification of all rights and obligations in relation to employees transferring to the transferee (see 4.1).

The regulations do not, however, specify in what form the information disclosed under reg. 10 should take and so original documentation cannot be demanded. There is also no requirement to supply all supporting documentation, although additional documentation can be demanded by the appropriate representatives if it is necessary for meaningful negotiations to take place.

4.3   EMPLOYEES AFFECTED

All affected employees must be informed under reg. 10(1), which states that 'affected employees' means not only employees who are to be transferred along with the new business to a new employer, but any other employee of the transferor or of the transferee who may be affected by the transfer or who may be affected by 'measures taken' in connection with the transfer. 'Taking measures' is also not defined but it can encompass any significant alteration in existing working practices. The duty is therefore to provide information not only to employees who transfer but also to those who will not transfer but who will be affected by the transfer. The transferee will also be under an obligation to provide information to its own employees who will be affected by the transfer of new employees into its business. In some circumstances employers may be under a duty to consult with all of their employees about a transfer.

The only limitation on the word 'affected employee' is that it is restricted to employees of the relevant employer. Employees of associated employers are not affected employees.

4.4   TIMING OF CONSULTATION

Under TUPE reg. 10(2) the duty on the employer is to provide information in sufficient time before the transfer to enable consultation to take place. Regulation 10(2)(a) states that appropriate representatives must be given information about the 'fact that the relevant transfer is to take place'.

Under reg. 10(8) employee representatives are entitled to be consulted by the employer 'as soon as reasonably practicable after the election of the representatives'. There is no specific timetable for the provision of information under the TUPE regulations, but case law has now developed this area to provide some guidelines. The fact that employees fail to elect representatives where there is no recognised trade union does not mean that the employer can avoid informing and consulting or that employees can delay a transfer. Regulation 10(8A) clearly states that where employees fail to elect appropriate representatives within a reasonable time, the employer must give all the information to each affected employee.

In *Banking Insurance and Finance Union* v. *Barclays Bank plc* [1987] ICR 495 it was held that the duty to inform is triggered where there is a proposed or planned transfer, even if it does not take place, and in *Institution of Professional Civil Servants* v. *The Secretary of State for Defence* [1987] IRLR 373, [1987] 3 CMLR 35 it was stated that information must be given in good time to enable voluntary consultations to take place even if no consultations are required by statute.

Although the TUPE regulations require a minimum period of information and consultation, it would be a mistake to leave this until the last minute. Consultation with employee representatives must take place with a view to reaching agreement and this can only be achieved if sufficient time is given for this statutory process to be meaningful. Although no specific timetable is suggested by the regulations, the information must be supplied long enough before a transfer to allow for the duty to consult to be performed. The timetable could be anything between one week to three months, depending upon the size structure and complexity of the workforce.

4.5 DUTY TO CONSULT

The duty to provide information applies to every transfer but the duty to consult only arises where the relevant employer envisages that it will be taking measures in relation to any of its affected employees. The duty is to consult the appropriate representatives in respect of that category of employee. Under TUPE reg. 10(5) the duty to consult shall be taken with a view to 'seeking agreement to measures to be taken'.

An onerous duty is therefore placed upon the employer to show that a genuine attempt has been made to inform, consult and reach agreement in relation to any measures that are proposed. Consultation need not take place, however, until it is clear that measures will be taken. There is no duty to consult about mere possibilities.

The transferor is obliged to consult with the appropriate representatives of its own employees in relation to whom it envisages that it will be taking measures either before or after the transfer. The transferor does not have to consult with representatives of employees who will transfer as it will be the transferee who will be proposing to take measures in relation to them after the transfer. The only duty in relation to the transferring of employees is to provide the appropriate representatives with information concerning measures the transferee envisages that it will take.

The transferee will be obliged to consult with the appropriate representatives of the transferring employees once the transfer has taken place. Regulation 10(5) does not require them to consult with such representatives prior to the transfer taking place as it states that:

> Where an employer of any affected employee envisages that he will, in connection with the transfer, be taking measures in relation to any such employees he shall consult all the persons who are appropriate representatives of any of the affected employees in relation to whom he envisages taking measures with a view to seeking agreement to measures to be taken.

There is therefore a void in the consultation procedure for transferring employees in respect of measures being taken after the transfer as it only obliges the employer to consult about the measures that it will be taking. If the measures are to be taken by the transferee, the persons who will transfer will not be the employees of the transferee when the consultation should take place, i.e. before the transfer. The only practical way to overcome this problem is to ensure that the transferee company attends meetings at the transferor's premises to meet with the transferring employees before the transfer takes place in order to provide information and consult with the employees regarding measures that are to be taken after the transfer.

Under reg. 10(5) the duty to consult only arises where the employer envisages that it will be taking measures. If no measures are to be taken, no consultation need take place (*IPCS* v. *Secretary of State for Defence* (see above, p.57)). Measures were defined in the above case as including 'any action, step or arrangement'. The duty to consult applies only where there are definite plans, which must be related to the transfer. This would exclude matters that are a mere possibility. It would also exclude measures to be taken that are not directly related to the transfer. Whether or not a measure is directly related to the transfer is down to evidence, but if an employer gets this wrong and fails to inform and consult on certain information, the mistake may be costly.

The obligation to consult relates only to the nature of the proposed measures, even though the information that is to be provided under reg. 10(2) is wider than that. Interestingly enough, there is presently no obligation on the employer to consult with appropriate representatives about the fact that the transfer is to take place or concerning the reasons for the transfer, but this will change when Directive 2002/14/EC comes into force in the UK.

The purpose of consultation under TUPE reg. 10(5) states that consultation must be undertaken 'with a view to seeking the appropriate representatives' agreement of the measures to be taken'. This does not state that agreement must be reached, but there must be evidence to show that the parties made a genuine attempt to reach agreement. If an employer cannot show an attempt was made to reach agreement, this may be evidence of a failure to consult. Regulation 10(6) further clarifies that during consultation the employer must consider representations made by appropriate representatives and reply to those representations. If the employer rejects those representations it must state the reason for doing so. It is therefore clear that the duty on the employer is to provide the appropriate representatives with sufficient information upon which to consult and then to consult with them and thereafter to respond where appropriate. There is also a duty to provide the appropriate representatives with access to the affected employees and to facilities and accommodation as may be appropriate under reg. 10(6A). This is clearly designed to facilitate open communication, information and consultation.

It is essential that the transferor complies with the duty to inform and consult, as the remedies available to employees and appropriate representatives do not transfer to the transferee after the transfer. The case law on this point is *Angus Jowett and Company v. The National Union of Tailors and Garment Workers* [1985] IRLR 326, EAT. If there has been a failure by the transferor to carry out this obligation and it wishes to avoid liability to pay any sums due in respect of claims arising, it would be advised to obtain an indemnity from the transferee. This will be a necessity if the failure to consult arose out of the transferee's failure to provide the transferor with the relevant information upon which to consult and inform.

If there has been a failure by the transferor to inform and consult, it is clear from reg. 12 that any compromise agreement will be void if it attempts to preclude an employee's right to present a claim to the employment tribunal:

> Any provision in any agreement (whether a contract of employment or not) shall be void in so far as it purports to exclude or limit the operation of Regulation 5, 8, or 10 above or to preclude any person from presenting a complaint to an employment tribunal under Regulation 11.

There has been one case in this area dealing with the responsibility placed upon the transferor when performing its duty to inform and consult. This is the case of *Howard Hagen* v. *ICI Chemicals and Kvaemer Engineering* (19 October 2001). Central Engineering of ICI was transferred to the transferee, Redpath Engineering Ltd. The transfer took place in 1994. ICI complied with its obligation to consult with recognised trade unions. The workforce did not wish to transfer because the policy of ICI was to avoid redundancies; the employees therefore had to be persuaded to transfer, since for the transfer to be viable all of the employees had to transfer to the transferee. During a consultation meeting, ICI misrepresented the value of the transferees' pension scheme, saying that it would be within half a percent of the ICI scheme. This was not correct and the mistake was not corrected by the transferee, whose representatives were in the meeting at the time.

The judge implied that there was a duty on ICI within the contract of employment to take reasonable care in making statements where the employer was proposing that the employees transfer their employment, where the transfer would affect the future economic interests of the employees, where the transfer was unlikely to take place if a significant body of the employees objected, where the employer had access to certain information unavailable to employees and where it knew that this information or advice would carry considerable weight with the employees. The employer therefore owed a tortious duty towards its employees in informing and consulting about a proposed transfer.

The cheapest and most effective way of approaching this obligation is to accord with it.

4.6 APPROPRIATE REPRESENTATIVES

Employers are obliged to inform and consult with appropriate representatives of their own employees who may be affected by the transfer or measures that will be taken in connection with such transfer. 'Appropriate representative' is defined in reg. 10(2A). Appropriate representatives are representatives of an independent trade union which is recognised by the employer. Where affected employees are not members of a recognised union the employer can choose to consult with the following:

(a) employees who have been appointed or elected by the affected employees otherwise than for specific purposes of this regulation who (having regard to the purposes for and the method by which they were appointed or elected) have authority from those employees to receive information and to be consulted about the transfer on their behalf; or

(b) employees elected by the affected employees for the specific purpose of being given information or being consulted by the employer under the requirements of the Regulations in an election satisfying TUPE reg. 10A.

Employers therefore do not now have an option of choosing whether or not to consult with a recognised trade union. The only way to avoid consulting with a recognised trade union is to derecognise it under the Employment Relations Act 1999. If this were done the entire collective bargaining procedure would have to be dismantled. The employer can only choose whom to inform and consult if there is no recognised union for the affected employees. In such circumstances the employer can either choose to negotiate with a workplace representative or with representatives who have been elected for the specific purpose of consulting under TUPE.

Where there is no recognised trade union, the employer will need to ask the employees whether they wish to appoint an appropriate representative to receive information and consult with the employer on their behalf under the provisions of the TUPE regulations. If the employees choose to elect an appropriate representative, certain steps must be followed. The election procedures are set out in reg. 10A. They specify that:

(a) the employer must make such arrangements as are reasonably practicable to ensure that the election is fair;

(b) the employer may determine the classes of employees for whom representatives are to be elected, the number of representations and their term of office;

(c) candidates for election as employee representatives must be employees affected by the transfer and no affected employee may be unreasonably excluded from standing for election;

(d) all affected employees on the date of the election are entitled to vote for appropriate representatives;

(e) affected employees may vote for as many candidates as there are representatives;

(f) as far as reasonably practicable, an employer must ensure that affected employees can vote in secret and that votes are accurately counted; and

(g) if a representative once elected ceases to act as such, a further election must be held to appoint a replacement where employees would otherwise be underrepresented.

If employees fail to elect representatives within a reasonable time, the employer must give to each affected employee the information that it would otherwise give to the appropriate representatives. It must be a matter of common sense for employers and employees to reach a consensus as to whether it is necessary to appoint an appropriate representative. Small employers may not need to appoint representatives where communications are conducted on a daily basis to individual employees, throughout the company.

Once elected, all appropriate representatives are given protection under TUPE, including:

(a) access to all affected employees;
(b) access to such accommodation and facilities as may be appropriate (reg. 10(6A));
(c) the right to claim automatic unfair dismissal and victimisation arising out of dismissals or any detriment suffered as a consequence of acting as an appropriate representative or taking part in an election for an appropriate representative; and
(d) the right to time off work with pay in order to train for and undertake duties as an appropriate representative.

4.7 HIVING DOWN

It was felt inappropriate that the TUPE regulations should apply to hiving off situations where receivers, administrators or liquidators transfer the salvageable part of a company to a subsidiary in order to sell it off and to protect jobs and to find buyers for businesses. Allowing the regulations to apply in such situations would make any package put together by an insolvency practitioner unattractive as it would have too many strings attached. Hiving down is therefore treated as a special case under reg. 4 where there will only be deemed to be one transfer that being from the administrator, receiver or liquidator to the ultimate purchaser. The administrator, liquidator or receiver is manager and transferor of the company and should inform or consult with unions about a transfer to the ultimate purchaser.

However, tribunals will investigate elaborate transactions that are put in place with the sole objective of avoiding the effects of the regulations. The tribunals see their role, where elaborate measures are put in place, to 'penetrate the facade of the labyrinth provisions sometimes found in agreements for sale made by receivers, administrators and liquidators to determine the real effect and intention behind them'.

The courts are also critical of receivers who fail to take any steps to inform and consult as can be seen in the case of *Kerry Foods Ltd* v. *Creber* [2000] IRLR 10, EAT where receivers of a company dismissed staff within seven days of them being appointed and transferred the business to Kerry Foods. EAT criticised the receivers for failing to comply with an obligation to consult with appropriate representatives under TUPE, stating that it had been reasonably practicable. The EAT also stated that when a receiver is appointed with a view to selling a business, the obligation to consult arises on his or her appointment, however many employees may be involved. It was of cardinal importance that receivers consulted with staff at the earliest possible opportunity. An award of four weeks' compensation was made.

In the public consultation document published by the Department of Trade and Industry on the 1 October 2001 it has now been confirmed that the government believes that in light of the above case law and of its proposals to take advantage of the new derogations in the Directive (see Appendix 1) the existing provisions in reg. 4 of the regulations relating to hiving down no longer serve any useful purpose.

It is now looking at ways of developing a viable rescue culture where a business is insolvent and is subject to compulsory winding up, bankruptcy and possibly creditors voluntary winding up. The two options are at present under the consultation document is that either the transferor's previous debts towards the employees do not pass to the transferee or employers and employee representatives can agree to change the terms and conditions of employment as long as the changes are:

(a)   agreed;
(b)   designed to safeguard employment opportunities; and
(c)   not contrary to UK law.

It is now proposed to remove the provisions relating to hiving down from the TUPE regulations.

Any changes that are made to the insolvency provisions must take into account art. 5(4) of the Directive which clearly directs all member states to prevent the misuse of insolvency proceedings being used to deprive employees of the rights of the Directive. More clarification of this point in UK domestic jurisdiction should be issued shortly.

4.8 REMEDIES AVAILABLE TO APPROPRIATE REPRESENTATIVES

Where an employer fails to comply with the duty to inform and consult, the appropriate representatives can make a complaint to the employment tribunal. Complaints can be made to the employment tribunal the following grounds (see reg. 11(1)):

(a) regarding the election of appropriate representatives by any affected employee;
(b) relating to appropriate representatives by the representatives to whom the failure relates;
(c) relating to trade union representatives by the trade union concerned; and
(d) on any other matter by an affected employee.

However, an affected employee cannot make a complaint that the appropriate representative is not doing his or her job properly. The only cause of action is against the employer in respect of failure to comply with its duties under reg. 10 and reg. 10A (failure to provide information to consult and failure to consult and failure to comply with requirements concerning the election of appropriate representatives).

Complaints must be submitted within three months beginning with the date of the transfer. The remedy sought is a declaration (reg. 11(4)). Where the employment tribunal makes a declaration to the effect that the employer is under a duty to inform and consult under the TUPE regulations and the employer still fails to do so, a further complaint may be made to the tribunal concerning that failure. If the tribunal still finds the complaint to be well founded, it may order the employer to pay compensation to the employee.

The tribunal can also award compensation to be paid to the employee by the employer. This will usually be an award against the transferor employer unless the transferor has managed to pass the obligation to pay the award on to the transferee by way of an indemnity.

The compensation that can be awarded is up to 13 weeks' gross pay for each affected employee. The level of award to be paid is that which the tribunal considers to be just and equitable 'having regard to the seriousness of the failure of the employer to comply with his duty'. The award may be made in addition to payments made in lieu of notice and other contractual payments or awards that can be made by the employment tribunal.

4.9 DEFENCES

Where a complaint is lodged about the failure of a transferor to inform appropriate representatives about measures to be taken, it is a defence to say that the transferee failed to provide the transferor with all the information. If this defence is to be used, the transferor must serve notice on the transferee to join it as a party to the proceedings. The transferee will then be liable under reg. 11(3) (see the cases of *Unison* v. *P B Kennedy and Dunkin Ltd, Unicorn Consultancy Services Ltd* v. *Westbrook* [2000] IRLR 80, EAT).

The employer also has a defence that there were special circumstances which rendered it not reasonably practicable for it to perform the duty and that it took all the steps towards its performance that were reasonably practicable in those circumstances (reg. 11(2)). There is no definition of 'special circumstances' and the only guidance forthcoming has been from case law. They have been defined in cases as 'being something unforeseen or unexpected' (*Clarks of Hove* v. *Bakers Union* [1978] IRLR 366). The employer must also show it was not reasonably practicable for it to comply or fully comply with its obligations due to these special circumstances. Whether that is so or not has to be decided by an objective assessment of the situation (*Union of Construction and Allied Trades and Technicians* v. *H Rooke and Sons Ltd* [1978] IRLR 204).

4.10 ADVICE TO TRANSFERORS AND TRANSFEREES

In order to comply with all the TUPE regulations on informing and consulting, it is recommended that the following be taken into consideration:

1. As soon as a transfer situation arises, time must be allowed in the process of the sale or the transfer of the business to inform and consult.

2. When deciding how long it will take to inform and consult it is necessary to identify the affected employees of both the transferor and the transferee. Affected employees are employees whose activities, responsibilities and working arrangements will be affected by the transfer. It is then necessary to consider whether appropriate representatives need to be elected or if the employees are represented by a recognised trade union. If

appropriate representatives need to be elected then the following procedures need to be put in place:

(a) employees need to be informed of their right to elect a representative (see draft letter no. 1 in Appendix 5);

(b) arrangements need to be put in place for nominations to be put forward by the affected employees (see draft no. 2);

(c) ballot arrangements need to be set up. The ballot must be secret and votes must be accurately counted (see draft form no. 3);

(d) facilities must be set up for appropriate representatives to advise their employees;

(e) training must be given to allow the representatives to fulfil their obligations under the regulations;

(f) information must then be supplied to the appropriate representatives;

(g) consultation should then take place with a view to seeking agreement. At least two meetings should be scheduled, the first to discuss the information and to take questions, the second to reply to any representations made by the representatives (see draft form no. 4).

3. Papers relating to the nomination and election of appropriate representatives (if necessary) and ballot papers must be kept for a minimum of at least four to six months after election. All papers relating to the information and consultation stage should also be kept for this period.

4. It is necessary to provide information to appropriate representatives in sufficient time before the transfer to allow for meaningful consultation to take place. If there are no appropriate representatives, or the employees fail to elect a representative, then the obligation is to inform and consult with individual employees.

This duty is placed upon the transferor to inform and consult in respect of employees to be transferred; therefore the transferor must ask the transferee for any details of any measures the transferee envisages taking after the transfer in relation to transferring employees. The transferor must then pass this information to the affected employees or their appropriate representatives. The transferor must also provide to the transferee all the details of the employees who are transferring and their contractual terms and conditions of employment and personnel details in writing. The obligation to inform is on the employer under the TUPE regulations and therefore the transferor has a duty to provide the information to employees who will transfer in respect of changes to be made after the transfer.

5. Consultation must be undertaken with a view to seeking agreement. The employer must be seen to be consulting and responding to the representations made by the employees. If the employer rejects any representations, reasons must be given in support of those decisions. The entire consultation process should be conducted (or evidenced) in writing. There should also be a minimum of two meetings to show that effective consultation has taken place and to allow feedback and adequate responses to be delivered to the employee or employer.

Consideration should be given as to whether the transferee should be allowed to attend the consultation process. There are benefits from the industrial relations point of view, as this is an excellent way for the transferee to speak to and to obtain feedback from prospective employees. It also allows employees to decide, after proper consultation, whether they wish to transfer or whether they would prefer to object to the transfer and resign. The employees may wish to consider claiming constructive dismissal under reg. 5(5) (see 5.14 and 5.15) arising from the identity of the transferee. It is only at the consultation stage that employees have an opportunity of making their views known after having access to full information.

6. If the transfer takes place by agreement, the terms of transfer must contain indemnities in respect of claims from employees dismissed for a reason connected with the transfer or after the transfer. If the transferee wishes to make detrimental changes to the contracts of employment of those employees who transfer indemnities will also have to be considered. These indemnities should be cross-indemnities by both the transferor and transferee (see Appendix 6).

It is important to remember that an employer cannot avoid the duty to inform and consult. The most prudent and cost effective approach to adopt is to fulfil the duty. By carrying out the duty to inform and consult, the transfer is likely to take place without any problems and claims in respect of a failure under this section will be avoided or mitigated.

7. In outsourcing arrangements, where there is a new contractor, and the employees are expected to take on new duties and roles, it is essential that the original transferor ensures that the original transferee and any subsequent transferees are obliged to provide

information to subsequent contractors to comply with their obligation to inform and consult with affected employees under the regulations.

4.11 ADVISING EMPLOYEES

At the pre-transfer stage, employees have a right to be informed and consulted. When advising employees in connection with the transfer the following issues have to be considered:

1. If the employee is a member of a recognised trade union, the trade union has a right to be consulted on behalf of its members. Employees who are not trade union members have a right to elect appropriate representatives to consult on their behalf. Employees also have a right to be informed and consulted individually if they are not represented by either form of representative.

2. All employees who may be affected by the transfer are entitled to be informed about it. This would apply to employees of both the transferor and the transferee. The information that must be provided must accord with that outlined in reg. 10(2).

3. Where the transferee decides to 'take measures' in relation to its employees, including those whom it employs and those who will transfer to it, information must be provided to the recognised trade unions and to the appropriate representatives of the transferor's as well as the transferee's employees. Consultation then must take place with a view to reaching agreement. All employees are therefore entitled to ask for documentation and information and to have input into the proposals. If no feedback is forthcoming from the transferor or the transferee following representations, this may be prima facie evidence that effective consultation has not taken place.

4. Those who agree to act as appropriate representatives are protected from unfair dismissal and victimisation. They are also allowed facilities and time off in which to carry out their duties. Appropriate representatives have a right of action against the employer, if they have a complaint in connection with the employer's failure to allow an election to chose appropriate representatives or out of an employer's failure to provide facilities.

    Where facilities are provided, it is essential to ensure that any telephone lines are confidential and any emails sent for this purpose are secure. Failure to provide confidential telephone lines or email facilities could be a breach of the Human Rights Act 1998 and the Regulation of Investigatory Powers Act 2000.

An employee has a right to time off with pay to perform the duties as appropriate representative; such representatives also have a right to receive training. If the person performing that role is a trade union representative, this training will usually be undertaken by the union. This is where recognised union status works to the benefit of the employer.

5. All employees can complain to the employment tribunal in respect of the transferor's or transferee's duty to inform or consult. The remedy is either a declaration and/or compensation. The compensation can be up to 13 weeks' gross pay. All claims are lodged and enforced against the transferor.

6. When the transferor provides information to the transferee, these disclosures will be subject to the provisions of the Data Protection Act 1998. In order to comply with the provisions of the Act, it has been suggested in the Code of Practice that, where possible, all information on employees that is disclosed during the negotiations should be anonymised. Where it is not possible to do this, when the information relates to a key employee, conditions should be attached to the release of that information. These conditions should include the following:

(a) the information should only be used for the purposes of the negotiations;
(b) it must be kept secure;
(c) it must not be disclosed to any third parties;
(d) it must be destroyed if the business sale does not proceed.

When advising key employees then it is important to alert them of their rights under the Data Protection Act to protect the security of their files and to ensure that their contents are not disclosed to others outside the negotiations. It is also important for employees to establish that the contents of their personnel files are accurate. Civil and criminal sanctions can be invoked in respect of breaches of the Data Protection Act. Under s.13 of the Act, individuals have a right to compensation if they suffer damage as a result of a breach committed by a person who controls their data.

Where employees are transferred, all personnel records should be transferred to the transferee. However, all employees should be given an opportunity to check the accuracy of the information before it is passed on to the new employer. All employees should be given an opportunity to do this and to correct any inaccuracies on their file. An employer is entitled to make a charge for an employee to gain access to their personnel files and that charge presently stands at £10 but employers must provide access to the information promptly and in any event within 40 days of receiving the request.

When advising employees, it should also be considered whether the action of the employer amounts to a potential breach of contract or the employer's implied duty of mutual trust and confidence as well as a breach of the TUPE regulations.

CHAPTER 5

Consideration of the employment relationship

5.1 BEFORE TUPE

Before the TUPE regulations came into force, it was a fundamental principle of English law that an employment contract could not be transferred to another person without the employee's consent. TUPE reg. 5 changed that rule. A contract of employment made by the employee with the transferor could now, on completion of the transfer, be transferred to the transferee irrespective of the employee's wishes. Regulation 5 provided for the automatic continuation of the contract without the need for the consent of the employee. The transfer of a contract to a transferee did not therefore amount to a repudiatory breach entitling an employee to apply for injunction to prevent the transfer (*Newns* v. *British Airways plc* [1992] IRLR 575, CA).

5.2 EFFECT OF TUPE REGULATION 5

TUPE reg. 5(1) makes it clear that the transfer of an undertaking does not terminate a contract of employment but instead the contract is transferred to a transferee. Regulation 5(1) only applies to a contract which comes to an end as a result of actions of the transferor. The regulations do not operate:

(a) if the contract would otherwise have been preserved (express agreement or re-negotiation);

(b) if the contract is terminated otherwise than by the transfer (for example misconduct and/or case of capability, etc.);

(c) if the contract is of fixed term duration and expires prior to the transfer. However, art. 2(2)(b) of Directive 2001/23/EC provides that contracts of employment shall not be excluded solely because they are of fixed term duration. This is likely to become law soon in the form of the Fixed Term Workers Regulations; or

(d) if the transferor retains an employee to work in part of the business which is not being transferred.

The TUPE regulations state as follows:

Regulation 5

(1) except where objection is made under paragraph (4(A) below, a relevant transfer shall not operate so as to terminate the contract of employment of any person employed by the Transferor in the undertaking or part transferred but any such contract which would otherwise have been terminated by the transfer shall have effect after the transfer as if originally made between the persons employed and the Transferee.

(2) Without prejudice to paragraph (1) above subject paragraph 4(A) below on the completion of the relevant transfer–

(a) all the Transferor's rights, powers, duties and liabilities under or in connection with any such contract can be transferred by virtue of this regulation to the Transferee; and

(b) anything done before the transfer is completed by or in relation to the Transferor in respect of that contract or person employed in that undertaking or part shall be deemed to have been done by or in relation to the Transferee.

(3) Any reference to paragraph (1) or (2) above to a person employed in an undertaking or part of one transferred by a relevant transfer is a reference to a person so employed immediately before the transfer, including, where the transfer is effected by a series of two or more transactions, a person so employed immediately before any of those transactions.

(4) Paragraph (2) above shall not transfer or otherwise affect the liability of any person to be prosecuted for, convicted of and sentenced for any offence.

5.3 EMPLOYMENT IN THE PART TRANSFERRED

It is important to establish whether an employee was employed in the part transferred because if so reg. 5 will operate to transfer the contract to the transferee. If the employee was not employed in the part transferred, the rights will not be so transferred and the employee's only rights will be against the transferor in respect of any dismissals or contractual changes. This can be seen in the two cases of *Michael Peters Limited* v. *Farnfield and Michael Peters Group plc* [1995] IRLR 190, EAT. The chief executive of Michael

Peters Group plc, a holding company for 25 consultancies, was responsible for the financial management of all subsidiaries. Receivers were appointed to the parent company and the chief executive was made redundant. A day later four subsidiaries were sold. The chief executive brought an unfair dismissal complaint, arguing that the four subsidiaries together were the parent company's assets and together constituted a single economic unit so when it was transferred the TUPE regulations applied. It was held that it was wrong to pierce the corporate veil. The parent company was not the transferor and the employee was not employed by the transferor nor was he assigned or allocated to a part of the undertaking that was transferred.

However, it is a question of fact whether employees are employed in the part transferred, where they work for more than one company in the group, as seen in the case of *Sunley Turriff Holdings Limited* v. *Thomson* [1995] IRLR 184, EAT. Here an employee was the company secretary and chief accountant of the main company and its subsidiary. His contract of employment was with the main company, but his job included work for the subsidiary. Receivers were appointed over both companies and the subsidiary was sold. It was admitted that there was a transfer of the subsidiary to the transferee and a substantial amount of the employee's work was concerned with the part that was transferred. The employee was not included on the list of employees and did not transfer with the company, but was retained in that part that was retained by the receivers. EAT approved of the tribunal's action in lifting the corporate veil and finding that the contract had been transferred to the transferee. The employment tribunal was entitled to find that the employee was assigned to the part of the undertaking which was transferred.

Guidance upon how to apply the test of whether an employee is 'assigned to the part of the group transferred' was considered in *Duncan Web Offset (Maidstone) Limited* v. *Cooper* [1995] IRLR 633, EAT. In this case, one of a group of companies was in liquidation. The company was sold and the employees who had not been taken on by the buyer did notionally transfer (to the extent of liability for their claims), principally as a result of the amount of work that they had done for that particular company. The EAT held that they had been assigned to that part of the group. It then went on to discuss how to reach a conclusion as to whether an employee had been assigned to the part transferred. In this discussion (which was *obiter*) three scenarios were discussed.

The first scenario

A Company transferred part of a business to B Company. All the relevant factors had to be looked at to see if the employee had been assigned to that part of the undertaking that had been transferred. The test of *Botzen* v. *Rotterdamsche Droogdok Maatschappij BV* (C-186/83) [1986] 2 CMLR 50, ECJ was applied. In this case, the ECJ put forward the following guidance to assist with the determination of whether an employee was assigned to a business and thus was transferred with the business. The list is not deemed to be exhaustive or comprehensive:

(a)   the time spent on one part of the business or another;
(b)   the amount of value given to each part by the employee;
(c)   the terms of the contract of employment showing what the employee could be required to do;
(d)   how the cost to the employer of the employee's services had been allocated between the different parts of the business.

The second scenario

Company A employed an employee to work on Company B's business. Company B transferred the business to Company C. The TUPE regulations would not apply to transfer the employee from B to C as the employee was employed by A and not by B and the employee would revert to A. The tribunal should look carefully to see whether the corporate structures and service companies were being used to evade the regulations.

The third scenario

Company A comprised a group of companies employing people who worked for companies within the group. A transferred one of its subsidiaries to B. Employees working in that subsidiary would normally go with the transfer unless the amount of work done by the employee for other companies in the group was so great that the employee would not transfer on the grounds that he or she had not been assigned to the part of the business that had been transferred. Whether there had been an effective transfer could not be determined by looking at the contractual tests alone (see *Michael Peters* above). The tribunal should consider the protective purposes of the Directive and not allow corporate structures to get in the way of the Directive as a whole.

5.4   CONTRACTS CONTAINING MOBILITY CLAUSES

If a contract contains a mobility clause, can the transferee argue that the employee cannot be employed in the part transferred? This was put forward unsuccessfully in *Securicor Guarding Limited* v. *Fraser Services Limited* [1996] IRLR 552, EAT. The facts of the case were that employees were employed to guard a particular site. Although the employees' contracts of employment contained a mobility clause, they had never been asked to move or to work on any other site. When Securicor's contract ended, it was put up for retender. Securicor lost and the new contractor denied that the TUPE regulations applied and offered work to the employees at a substantially lower rate of pay. The new contractor argued that as there was a mobility clause, the employees were not employed in the part transferred. The court held that the employees were employed in the part transferred, despite the fact that contractually they could have been asked to work on any site within a reasonable travelling distance. The TUPE regulations applied and the employees' claim was not negatived by the mobility clause.

The only way in which a mobility clause would prevent TUPE applying to employees' contracts would be if the transferor moved the employees to a site that was not transferred before the transfer took place. Under those circumstances, the employees would not be assigned to the part transferred immediately before the transfer.

5.5   IMMEDIATELY BEFORE THE TRANSFER

In order to be protected by TUPE, the regulations state at reg. 5(3) that the contracts of those persons employed 'immediately before the transfer' are preserved. But what do these words mean? Where a business is sold or transferred, the purchaser of that business will often wish to pick and choose the employees that it wishes to take with the business. However, the regulations will operate to preserve all contracts of those employees not dismissed by the transfer or before the transfer. Regulation 5(1) preserves all contracts of employment that transferred from the transferor to the transferee and they are treated as if made with the transferee. Regulation 5(2) transfers all the liabilities of the transferor to the transferee. If a dismissal takes place before the transfer and is not connected to or related to the transfer, all employee rights will be against the transferor alone.

In order for the employee's contract to transfer across to the transferee, the employee must be employed 'immediately before the transfer'. There has been much litigation on the meaning of these words arising in part out of the fact that the TUPE regulation did not fully reflect the spirit and letter of the Directive. The following case law gives an indication of how to identify whether an employee's rights transfer across and whether the transferor or the transferee is responsible to the employee for any rights arising out of the contract of employment.

The UK courts at first took a restrictive view of the word 'immediately' to mean 'at the moment of transfer'. It then became clear that this could allow the TUPE regulations to be open to abuse. The Danish case of *Bork* (see below) was the first to adopt an 'anti-abuse' view in not allowing a transferor to dismiss employees in an effort to avoid the provisions of the Directive. The spirit of *Bork* was then reflected in the UK case of *Litster*, which inferred provisions into reg. 5(c) to ensure that if employees were unfairly dismissed for a reason relating to the transfer, they would be deemed to be employed 'immediately before the transfer', thus allowing such employees the benefit of TUPE. This is referred to as the 'purposive approach'.

In *Secretary of State for Employment* v. *Spence* [1986] ICR 651, CA, the company went into receivership and the workforce was dismissed on Monday morning. The business was then sold, and the workforce were re-employed on Tuesday morning under a new contract of employment. The employees submitted claims for redundancy payments against the state as the transferor was insolvent. The Secretary of State argued that the transferee should pay the redundancy payments.

This was rejected by the Court of Appeal as it held that reg. 5 applied only to contracts of employment subsisting at the moment of transfer. As the employees had been dismissed before the relevant transfer the contracts no longer subsisted at the moment of the transfer. Also, the reason for the dismissal was that there was no prospect of any work for the business unless the contract could be renegotiated. The reason for the dismissal was not connected with the transfer, so that reg. 8 did not render the dismissal unfair. The only matter for decision was whether the employees were employed 'immediately before the transfer'. Where, before the actual termination, employees' contracts are terminated for a reason which is unconnected with the transfer, the question of whether they are employed immediately before the transfer, cannot be made to depend upon the degree of proximity between the two events, except where they are so close as to be contemporaneous. If a contract did not subsist at the moment of transfer reg. 5(1) did not operate. This case was decided without reference to reg. 8(1).

Spence appeared to dilute the spirit and letter of the Directive by limiting the protection available to those who were employed 'at the moment of transfer'. Therefore it was not inconceivable that transferors and transferees could reach an agreement for the transferor to dismiss long enough before the transfer to make the TUPE regulations ineffective and to remove all the protection from employees.

The case of *P Bork International A/S (in liquidation)* v. *Foreningen af Arbejdsledere i Danmark* [1989] IRLR 41, ECJ was then decided. This was the first case on the Directive dealing with anti-avoidance. The case looked at two issues:

(a) the circumstances in which a transfer will be deemed to have taken place; and

(b) treatment of employees who are dismissed prior to the transfer but for a reason connected with it.

The facts of the case were that a veneer factory was leased to PBI. The lessor OTF gave notice of termination of the lease in December 1981 and PBI gave notice to all employees employed in the undertaking. The factory ceased operating from the 22 December 1981. On the 30 December 1981 a company called JL purchased the lease of the factory and took control of it from the 4 January 1982 and then re-employed half of the staff previously employed by PBI. Later on PBI sold stock, spare parts and furniture to JL. Following the transfer, some of the staff taken on by JL claimed that PBI obligations in respect of wages and holiday pay passed to JL as their new employer under the Directive.

The ECJ looked at the facts of the case and observed that, for an employee to be protected by the Directive, a contract of employment, or an employment relationship must be in existence at the date of the transfer. The European Commission submitted that the Directive deemed there to be an unlawful dismissal of employees still employed in the undertaking, at the time of the transfer, so that they would be covered by the Directive. As the employees were re-engaged, the transferee could not argue an ETO defence (see Chapter 6). The transfer therefore fell within the scope of the Directive and the dismissal of the employees who were re-engaged had no effect under the Directive. The Commission proposed that the ECJ should find that art. 4 of the Directive had to be interpreted as meaning that the parties could not prevent the Directive from applying to re-engaged workers who had been dismissed shortly before the transfer as the lessee had ceased to operate the undertaking.

The ECJ held that:

1. Although the Directive applied only to workers who had a current employment relationship or a contract at the date of the transfer, the question of whether such a relationship or contract existed had to be assessed under national law, but looking at the observance of the mandatory rules of the Directive concerning the protection of workers against dismissal by reason of the transfer.

2. Workers employed in the undertaking whose contract of employment had been terminated on a date before the transfer contrary to art. 4 had to be considered as still employed in the undertaking on the date of the transfer, with the consequence that the obligations of the transferor were transferred to the transferee in accordance with art. 3.

In assessing whether or not the only reason for the dismissal was the transfer, account must be taken of the objective circumstances in which dismissal occurred and the fact that it took place at a time close to the date of the transfer and that the workers were subsequently re-engaged by the transferee. The type of factual assessment needed to determine the applicability of the Directive was for the national courts to decide. The ECJ found that the Directive applied whenever there was a change in the natural or legal person responsible for operating the undertaking who entered into contractual obligations as an employer with the employees of the undertaking. Even where a transfer took place in two stages where the lease was retransferred by the lessee to the owner, which then transferred it to the new owner, this did not preclude it being a transfer under the Directive, provided the undertaking retained its identity.

In the case of *Bork* the undertaking retained its identity as the economic entity was still in existence as the operation was continued by the new owner carrying on the same or similar business. In order to determine whether these conditions existed all the factual circumstances of the case had to be taken into account, including whether tangible or intangible assets were transferred as well as a major part of the staff of the undertaking, the degree of similarity between activities before and after the transfer and the duration of any period of stoppage connected with the transfer.

Bork therefore confirmed that the spirit and intention of the Directive had to be followed. It also confirmed that a transfer does not, without more, constitute grounds for dismissal (unless the dismissal is for an ETO). The Directive renders ineffective a dismissal which is connected with the transfer. *Bork* further confirmed that a worker whose employment is terminated before the date of the transfer would be considered under the Directive still to be employed by the undertaking at the moment of the transfer so that the obligations of the employer would be transferred to the transferee.

To determine whether the reason for dismissal was the transfer itself, one must look at:

(a) objective circumstances;
(b) whether a dismissal took place on a date close to the actual transfer;
(c) whether the workers were re-engaged by the transferee.

The factual assessment is a matter for the national courts.

The case of *Bork* did not state that *Spence* was wrong, but it indicated that the interpretation that should be put on national regulations implementing the directive, and thus on TUPE reg. 8 (see Chapter 6) was that any dismissal connected with a transfer would be unfair and therefore such dismissals were ineffective. If they were ineffective an employee ineffectively dismissed would still be employed in the undertaking immediately before the transfer.

This approach was upheld in the UK case of *Litster* v. *Forth Dry Dock and Engineering Company Ltd* [1989] IRLR 161, HL. Here a dock was placed in hands of receivers. At 3.30 p.m. all workers were dismissed and at 4.30 p.m. the business was transferred. This was a sale of assets alone, the purchasers taking a new lease of the docks from the landlord. It was held by the House of Lords that what was transferred was an undertaking. It was held that the reg. 8(1) provisions stated that a dismissal by reason of a transfer was to be treated as an unfair dismissal. This involved reading reg. 5(3) as if there were inserted after the words 'immediately before the transfer' the words 'or would have been so employed if he had not been unfairly dismissed in the circumstances described in Regulation 8(1)'. These words were therefore read into reg. 5(3) in order to give full effect to the Directive.

The reasoning in *Litster* also then went on to consider the case of *Spence*, as it was held in that earlier case that the employment relationship must subsist up to the very moment of the transfer in order for reg. 5(1) to apply. This was correct on the facts as in that case the reason for the dismissal was an ETO and it therefore fell within reg. 8(2); the dismissals were therefore not automatically unfair under reg. 8(1), as they were not connected with the transfer. Had the dismissals been connected with the transfer, they would have been deemed to have been employed 'immediately before the transfer'. In the *Litster* case the dismissals were not to be automatically unfair since they were all for an ETO (see Chapter 6) as the employees had been dismissed following pressure from the bank to the receivers to stop paying wages.

The cases of *Litster* and *Spence* were considered in the recent case of *Thompson* v. *SCS Consulting Ltd and another* [2001] IRLR 801, EAT. Here a receiver was appointed who proceeded to dismiss 25 employees 11 hours before the transfer. The dismissal was on the grounds that the employees 'were not required for the operation of the business and that it would not be economically viable for the business to continue if the dismissed employees remained in the employ of the vendors'. It was held in this case that the business was overstaffed, inefficient and insolvent and could only be made viable if the workforce were reduced. This was an ETO. As the employees had been dismissed 11 hours before the transfer TUPE reg. 5 did not operate to transfer the rights and liabilities of the employees to the transferee. It was also decided in this case that the courts were also entitled to take into account any collusion between the transferor and the transferee. In the case of *Litster*, there was collusion but in the present case there was no collusion leading up to the dismissal. It was taken into account that had the transferee not been on the scene to purchase the business, all of the employees would have been dismissed. The dismissals were not undertaken to secure a sale. It was for that reason that reg. 5 did not operate to transfer the employees' rights and liabilities to the transferee and the transferee took the business unencumbered.

5.6 DISMISSALS FOR A REASON NOT RELATING TO THE TRANSFER

It is important to note that employees' contracts that are terminated for a reason other than the transfer itself do not fall within reg. 5 and are not therefore automatically unfair. So dismissals, for example, for misconduct or poor attendance would be subject to the s.98 Employment Rights Act 1996 test for fairness. These dismissals would not be for a reason relating to the transfer and under such circumstances the claim would be against a transferor alone. The transferee would not inherit any responsibility for such dismissals.

However, where the employee was employed 'immediately before a relevant transfer' and the dismissal was solely on the ground of the transfer of the undertaking, the employee's contract would transfer to the transferee, as seen in the case of *Litster*. The courts will also take into account any evidence of collusion leading up to the dismissals; devices adopted to avoid the TUPE provisions will therefore be looked at carefully.

5.7   TERMINATION OF A FIXED TERM CONTRACT

When a fixed term contract is due to expire on the day before an economic entity in which an employee works is to be transferred, the TUPE regulations will not apply unless:

(a)   the transferor or the transferee employer offers to renew the contract; or
(b)   the transferor offered a renewal and this was accepted by the employee before the expiry of the contract.

In relation to (a) above, as there is no contract in force at the time of the transfer, the transferee would have no obligation to accept responsibility for the employee. It would be the transferor alone who would need to consider the payment of any redundancy payments and the meeting of any claims for unfair dismissal should a claim be lodged. A dismissal by a termination of a fixed term contract may be held to be transfer related if the non-renewal was for a reason connected with the transfer. It should now be noted that art. 2(2)b of Directive 2001/23/EC provides that:

> Member States shall not exclude from the scope of this Directive contracts of employment or employment relationships solely because they are employment relationships governed by a fixed duration contract of employment within Article 1(1) of the Council Directive 91/383/EEC of the 25 June 1991 supplementing the measures to encourage improvements in the Health and Safety at work of workers with a fixed-duration employment relationship or a temporary employment relationship.

It may be that the courts will take a dim view of the use of fixed term contracts which terminate shortly before the transfer, seeing them as devices to avoid liability for those who do not transfer across with the undertaking. It is likely that before long we will see the Fixed Term Workers Regulations in force. These regulations will become law in October 2002. Once they becomes law, further protection will be offered to those on fixed duration contracts and it may be more difficult to justify the termination of a fixed term contract where it is connected with the transfer of an undertaking. Under the second scenario in (b) above, the fixed term contract would transfer across to the transferee as the contract would be in existence at the time of the transfer.

When an employee is dismissed for a reason connected with the transfer at any time before the transfer takes place, reg. 5 will operate but the contract itself will not transfer unless the transferee decides to re-engage the employee. When an employee is dismissed before the transfer it is only the liabilities of the transferor that transfer to the transferee, i.e. for example the liability to pay compensation for unfair dismissal, redundancy payments or any contractual payments. It is also still open to an employer to argue the defence of an ETO to escape liability for paying compensation for unfair dismissal – assuming, of course, that there had been an effective termination of the contract.

In *Harrison Bowden Ltd* v. *Bowden* [1994] ICR 186 EAT, administrative receivers were appointed and advertised the business for sale. The employees were dismissed on 31 January. From the 4 to 8 February negotiations for sale took place and employees went in to assist in the handing over of the business as a going concern. On 11 February employees were offered permanent employment and on 12 March employees dismissed. The new owner said that the employees who claimed did not have sufficient continuity of service to lodge a valid claim for unfair dismissal. The employees sought to rely on previous service with previous employers and the transferor. It was held that since the reason for the dismissal of the employees on the 31 January was for the proposed transfer the dismissal was automatically unfair. The employees were treated as employed up to the date of the transfer. The court applied the case of *Litster* in order to deem that the employment continued up until the date of the transfer on 8 February, with the consequence that when the employees were was taken on there was continuity of employment.

The EAT also stated that the same effect could be achieved by having regard to s.218 of the Employment Rights Act 1996, which states:

If a trade or business or an undertaking (whether or not established by or under an Act), is transferred from one person to another

(a) The period of employment of an employee in the trade or business or undertaking at the time of the transfer counts as a period of employment with the Transferee and

(b) The transfer does not break the continuity of the period of employment.

If the dismissal does fall within the definition of an ETO and is thereby not automatically unfair then the test of fairness is applied under the Employment Rights Act 1996, s.98(4). If the dismissal fails that test because, for example, of a lack of warnings and consultations and the failure to hold hearings and appeals against dismissal, the claim can only be pursued against the transferor.

It also appears that in order to claim unfair dismissal an employee must have the requisite length of service. There is here some conflict again between the Directive (art. 4), which is only concerned with the reason for the dismissal and whether it was connected with the transfer. However, it does state that member states may provide that specific categories of employee may not be covered by the rules governing protection in respect of dismissal. This means that those with less than one year's service will not have a claim in respect of unfair dismissal on the termination of their contracts for a reason relating to the transfer.

The employee must also have two years' continuous service before a redundancy payment can be claimed.

5.8 EXTENT OF TRANSFER UNDER TUPE REGULATION 5

Not only contractual terms transfer but all the transferors' rights and obligations 'under or in connection with' the contract of employment transfer. The transferee also assumes responsibility for acts done before the transfer, by or on behalf of the transferor. This only extends to civil liability not to criminal liability. Collective agreements will transfer as seen in the case of *Whent* v. *T Cartledge Ltd* [1997] IRLR 153, EAT. The employees worked under a contract that stipulated that their pay and conditions would be in accordance with an NJC agreement. Following a contracting out the transferee derecognised the trade union and the union advised its members that the collective agreement was no longer applicable. The employees argued that their pay was still linked to the NJC agreement and that they were therefore entitled to any subsequent pay increases negotiated. The employees claimed:

(a) that there was an incorrect statement of terms and conditions of employment contrary to the Employment Rights Act 1996, s.1;

(b) that unlawful deductions from wages, in the form of unpaid salary increased, had been made.

It was held that:

1. The transferee was bound by the terms in the employees' contract of employment, which stipulated that the rate of remuneration would be fixed in accordance with the NJC agreement.

2. Under reg. 5, the transferred employees' contracts transferred with the term dealing with setting their rates of remuneration. The fact that the transferee sought to withdraw from the collective agreement did not change the employees' individual contractual terms.

3. The transferee was able to renegotiate contractual terms but had failed to do so.

If the employer sought to renegotiate the terms and conditions of employment, it would have to provide the correct contractual notice to avoid claims for breach of contract and unfair dismissal. The new contracts would have to contain all of the old terms (save for the NJC term) together with recognition of continuous service in order to reduce the value of any prospective claim that an employee might have against the transferee arising out of the contractual changes. If the value of the claim was small, most employees would decide not to litigate as the cost and time expended in pursuing the matter would be far in excess of any benefit worthy of defending. If the benefit was of some value, it might be prudent to negotiate with the employees and to effect a change in the employees' contractual terms by way of a compromise agreement in order to ensure that no claims can be pursued after the agreement is signed (see Appendix 7).

Whent did not refer to the case of *Wilson* v. *St Helens Borough Council* (see below, p.121) which suggested that a renegotiation may not be appropriate as the TUPE regulations create a moratorium on detrimental changes to terms and conditions of employment for a reason connected with the transfer of the undertaking, rendering such changes ineffective even when they are agreed by the employee.

However, compare the case of *Whent* v. *Cartledge Limited* with the case of *Ralton and others* v. *Havering College of FHE* [2001] IRLR 738, EAT, where it was held that Silver Book terms (the collectively bargained terms and conditions of employment applying to teachers in further and higher education) were not binding upon the transferee. The facts of this case were that fixed and indefinite contracts of employment transferred to the transferee with Silver Book terms. After the transfer, all the employees transferred on to fixed term contracts, again subject to Silver Book terms. On the expiry of the first post-transfer fixed term contract, the employees were offered renewals but not on Silver Book terms. They were accepted by the employees but then a dispute arose, and the employees claimed that the transferee was in breach of the Directive. It was held by the EAT that the purpose of the Directive was to preserve existing terms and conditions. When a fixed term contract ends, an employer is not obliged to renew the contract on the same terms. The transferee would therefore not be bound to renew on the same terms, and for this reason none of the employees on renewal of their contracts could compel the transferee to renew with reference to collectively bargained terms and conditions of employment.

Profit share schemes

Where a profit share scheme is operated by the transferor, it has been held that the transferee is not expected to continue the scheme but must offer a scheme of substantial equivalence, as held in the case of *Mitie Managed Services Ltd* v. *French & others* (EAT 408/00, 12 April 2002). Prior to the transfer, the employees were entitled to share in their employer's profits. The EAT was called upon to decide whether or not the transferee employer was obliged to make payments to the employees calculated by reference to the transferors' profit share scheme. The employees sought a declaration under the Employment Rights Act 1996, s.11 that they should continue to enjoy the benefits of the scheme after the transfer.

The EAT held that it would be absurd to argue a strict interpretation of reg. 5 as it would lead to injustice to a transferee if the transferee were to provide a profit share scheme based upon the performance of the transferor company. The EAT did hold, however, that the employees' post-transfer entitlement should be to 'participation in a scheme of substantial equivalence but one which is free from unjust, absurd or impossible features'. That would mean introducing a new profit share scheme operating by reference to the transferee employee's entity. The EAT went on to say that if terms of the scheme could not be agreed, they could revert to the employment tribunal for a determination under the terms.

This case expanded on an *obiter* comment made in the case of *Unicorn Consultancy Services Ltd* v. *Westbrook & others* [2000] IRLR 80, EAT and also considered but distinguished the case of *Whent* v. *Cartledge*.

5.9 CLAIMS FOR DISCRIMINATION

What transfers across is more than the contract of employment, as was seen in the case of *DJM International Limited* v. *Nicholas* [1996] IRLR 76, EAT. This concerned an employee who was dismissed at the age of 60 by the transferor and was re-employed by the same employer on a part-time basis. The undertaking was then transferred to the transferee and the employee was dismissed for a reason relating to redundancy. She claimed that she had been discriminated against by being made to retire at the age of 60 by the transferor, and the claim was made against the transferee. The employee was held to be entitled to bring that claim against the transferee as reg. 5 (2)(b) provides that 'Anything done before the transfer and completed by ... the Transferor in respect of that contract or a person employed in that undertaking ... shall be deemed to be done by the Transferee'. The emphasis is upon the employment relationship as a whole.

5.10 CLAIMS ARISING OUT OF A FAILURE TO INFORM AND CONSULT

In the case of *Angus Jowett and Company* v. *The National Union of Tailors and Garment Workers* [1985] IRLR 326, EAT it was held that TUPE reg. 5 did *not* transfer any liability on the part of the transferor arising out of a breach of an obligation to inform and consult with a recognised trade union under s.188 of the Trade Union Labour Relations (Consolidation) Act 1992. The contract itself is transferred, and so are all implied or incorporated rights whether by statute or otherwise (for example, the equality clauses under the Equal Pay Act). See also the case of *Howard Hagen* v. *ICI Chemicals and Kvaemer Engineering* (19 October 2001) at p.90.

Continuity of employee representation

The public consultation document of the Department of Trade and Industry confirms that the Directive contains a requirement relating to continuity of employee representation where an undertaking is transferred and retains its autonomy under art. 6(1). In order to bring the TUPE regulations fully into line with the amended Directive the consultation document confirms that where a union recognition declaration is made by the Central Arbitration Committee (CAC) under the provisions introduced by the Employment Relations Act 1999, this will be preserved across on a transfer of an undertaking.

The revised Directive also contains a provision relating to the continuity of employee representation in cases where a transferred undertaking *does not* retain its autonomy. A situation may arise where a small independently managed business becomes, following a transfer, a department of a larger business with its own existing management structure. If the transferor and transferee had different employee representation arrangements, for example if the transferor recognised a trade union but the transferee did not, there might be a period of time following the transfer when the employees would lose their representation rights.

It is not clear at present what view the government will take on whether employee representation rights will transfer across and whether there will be any embargo period.

5.11 DUTY TO MAKE STATUTORY PAYMENTS

The case of *Secretary of State for Employment* v. *Anchor Hotel (Kippford) Ltd* [1985] IRLR 452, EAT concerned the transfer of statutory duties. The respondent agreed the sale of the hotel and part of the sale agreement was that it was to dismiss all employees before the transfer. This it did and it paid all the employees statutory redundancy. The respondent then sought to recover the statutory payments from the Secretary of State. The Secretary of State rejected the respondent's claim for a rebate on the basis that the purchasers were legally liable to make the redundancy payment. The duty to make the redundancy payment passed to the purchasers of the business on the date of the transfer in respect of employees employed immediately before the transfer. Liabilities and obligations in tort also transferred to the transferee. It is suggested that reg. 5(2) only transfers tortious liabilities in respect of employees and does not extend to liabilities owed to third parties.

5.12 TORTIOUS LIABILITY OF THE TRANSFEROR

The position of employees who are injured at work by the negligence or breach of a statutory duty of the employer was confirmed in the cases of *Bernardone* v. *Pall Mall Services Group and others*; *Martin* v. *Lancashire CC* [2000] IRLR 487, [2001] ICR 197, CA. It was held in these cases that the tortious liability of the transferor passed to the transferee where there was a transfer. That being the case, the benefit of any employer's liability insurance policy would also transfer over. The transferor had a vested or contingent right to recover from the insurers under a policy taken out in respect of liability to employees in the workplace; those rights should transfer across and there was nothing in the Directive or the TUPE regulations to prevent that from happening.

In the case of *Howard Hagen* v. *ICI Chemicals and Kvaemer Engineering* (19 October 2001) it was held that the transferor was under a duty of care in giving information to the workforce about the value of the transferee's pension scheme as compared to that of the transferor's own. It was under this duty of care even though it was under a statutory duty to provide the information. The transferee was also under a duty of care as to statements of fact, opinion and intention that were communicated to the workforce.

It was found that the only negligent statement that had been made by the transferors, ICI, related to the pension benefits which individuals would be entitled to receive from the transferee. While these were misrepresentations, there was no liability under contract as the negligence did not border on recklessness or gross indifference so as to cause the breakdown of trust and confidence. Had the correct information been given, under normal circumstances the employees would have objected to the transfer and pressed for an improvement in pension terms. The judge concluded that this would have been modified so that no employee would have been more than 2 per cent worse off under the transferee's scheme. It was held that tortious liability for acts done by the transferor before the transfer passed to the transferee as this was a liability which arose 'in connection with' a contract of employment within the meaning of the TUPE reg. 5(2)(a). This particular liability did not transfer as it related to misrepresentations in connection with a pension scheme, which were caught by the exclusion as to occupational pensions under reg. 7. The liability therefore remained with the transferor as liability to provide a pension scheme does not transfer to the transferee under reg. 5. Rights and obligations under or in connection with an occupational pension scheme are not automatically transferred to the transferee under reg. 5 by virtue of reg. 7.

The public consultation document of the Department of Trade and Industry which was published on 1 October 2001 (see Appendix 4) has clarified the situation relating to insurance whereby all employers are legally obliged to insure themselves against liability to employees for bodily injury or disease arising from their employment. The cases of *Howard Hagen* and *Bernadone* have now established that not only does liability to employees in tort transfer under the TUPE regulations, but also the benefit of insurances policies taken out by the transferor in compliance with the legal requirement for compulsory insurance. This enables the transferee to call on that insurance in respect of liabilities that arose before the transfer.

In the public consultation document it is now confirmed that the government considers that this position is satisfactory in respect of transfers between private sector employers. There is a problem, however, with public sector transfers to private sector employers as public sector employers are generally exempted from the requirement to effect insurance cover, and other than in the exceptional cases where they have insured themselves on a voluntary basis there is no cover to transfer. The government has now confirmed in the consultation paper that it proposes to introduce provisions for the transferor and the transferee to be jointly and severally liable for liabilities to employees for injury or disease arising from their pre-transfer employment in those cases where the transferor was a public sector employer exempt from the legal insurance requirements.

5.13 TRANSFEREE BECOMES PARTY TO THE EMPLOYMENT CONTRACT

When the transferee becomes a party to the contract that was originally negotiated with the transferor, there may be problems with the construction of the terms of the contract. In *Morris Angel and Son Ltd* v. *Hollande* [1993] IRLR 169, CA the business transferred and the managing director was employed by the transferee. Before the transfer, the managing director signed a covenant with the transferor that he would not directly or indirectly procure orders or do business with any person, firm or company which had at any time during the preceding year done business with the transferor's group. When the transferee took over the company the managing director was dismissed. Prior to dismissal, the transferee had been substituted for the transferor in the contract of employment. The transferee sought to enforce the covenant to restrain the director from doing business with any of the contacts he had had with the transferor's customers throughout the previous year.

It was held at first instance that no such injunction could be granted and the court would only grant an injunction in respect of the transferee's clients, which was no use to the transferee as it needed to restrict the director from approaching those clients that he had dealt with in his previous employment prior to the transfer. The case then went to the Court of Appeal and it was held that TUPE reg. 5(1) required the covenant to be read as if it were retrospectively concluded between the transferee and the employee, so the transferee was to be regarded as the owner of the undertaking transferred throughout the year preceding the termination of the director's employment. The Court of Appeal therefore granted the injunction in respect of the previous transferor's business and not the transferee's business. To give the clause any other construction would have made the restraint wider than the covenant in the employee's contract of employment at the time of the transfer, and any such change would have been void.

5.14 EMPLOYEES' RIGHT TO OBJECT TO THE TRANSFER

In *Katsikas* v. *Konstantinidis* (C-132/91) [1993] IRLR 179, ECJ the employee was a cook in a restaurant. The restaurant was sold but the cook refused to work for the new owner and was dismissed by the transferor. The employee sued the transferor for notice period money and allowances due and owing. The transferor argued that it was not liable for these as it was not the employer at the time of dismissal as by that time the restaurant had been transferred. The Directive did not oblige an employee to continue the relationship with the transferee and the objection prevented the contract from transferring to the transferee. In the German equivalent of the TUPE reg. 5, there was a duty to object to transferring if the employee did not wish to transfer, but there appeared to be no duty to object in the UK regulations.

An amendment to reg. 5 was therefore made by regs. 5(4A) and 5(4B) after this case to allow the employee to object to the transfer. Since that amendment, an employee has had a choice of whether or not to transfer. If employees decide not to transfer they are deprived of their rights without any recourse to any claims against either the transferor or the transferee.

The amended clauses read as follows:

> (4A) Paragraph (1) and (2) shall not operate to transfer his contract of employment and the rights, powers, duties and liabilities under or in connection with it if the employee informs the Transferor or Transferee that he objects becoming employed by the Transferee.
>
> (4B) When an employee so objects to the transfer of the undertaking or part in which he is employed shall operate so as to terminate his contract of employment with the Transferor but he shall not be treated, for any purpose, as having been dismissed by the Transferor.

It has been accepted that there is no right to transfer an employee to a new employer against his or her will – that would be repugnant to the principle of freedom to contract. Regulation 5 provides that an employee's contract of employment with the transferor will cease if the employee objects to being transferred, but the termination will not amount to a dismissal. The termination will operate as if the employee had resigned before the transfer, by way of a lawful summary termination. The obligation is upon the employee to notify the transferor of the objection to the transfer; no particular guidance is given as to how this objection should be conveyed (see below). The employee under these circumstances will lose all employment rights, including the right to claim unfair dismissal.

As there are no procedural requirements that must be adopted by the employee for informing the transferor or the transferee of this objection it could be made orally or in writing or by conduct. There is also no legal obligation for the transferring employer to inform the employee of the consequences of any objection. An objection by the employee to the transferor is likely to be communicated by word, deed or in writing. But when a transferor employer becomes aware that the employee is contemplating objecting to the transfer, it would be advisable for it to explain to the employee the consequences of so objecting. If the employee is determined to continue to object, the transferor should obtain written confirmation of this fact from the employee in terms that are suggested in the draft letter no. 5 in Appendix 5.

The case of *Hay* v. *George Hanson (Building Contractors) Ltd* [1996] IRLR 427, EAT shows the effect of an objection to transfer by an employee who believed that if he objected, he would be kept on by the transferor. The employee was a joiner in part of the council's undertaking that was transferred. The employee objected to the transfer and tried to stay with the council on other work and then tried to secure a redundancy package. The issue was whether the employee had done enough to object to the transfer to prevent his contract passing to the transferee. It was held that the employee's state of mind could be communicated by word or by deed or both so that an informal objection could be enough to comply with reg. 5 (4B). The tribunal had been entitled to find that the employee's contract had not transferred and he was therefore left with no rights. There was no obligation on either transferor or transferee to inform the employee of the consequences of his actions.

Lord Johnston, on the issue of withholding consent to the transfer, said:

> to protest in advance of a transfer, which could be construed to be objecting, would not amount to an objection, in our opinion in the terms of the Regulations, unless it is translated into an actual refusal to consent to transfer which, in turn, is communicated to the relevant person or persons, before the transfer takes place.

However, judicial concern about the way in which employees could expose themselves when objecting to transfer without realising the full legal implications of their actions in part explained the following decision in *Senior Heat Treatment Ltd* v. *Bell* [1997] IRLR 614, EAT. The case involved contracting out of work previously undertaken by relevant employees, which coincided with the expiry of a lease. The employees were given three choices:

(a)   alternative employment with the transferor;
(b)   transfer to the transferee with full protection of the TUPE regulations; or
(c)   to opt out of the regulations, in which case they would receive an agreed severance payment and statutory redundancy.

The relevant employees chose option (c) and had to sign a form saying that they did not wish to transfer to the transferee, but, on the same day signed a contract of employment with the transferee. They were dismissed 11 months later. They claimed unfair dismissal and redundancy against the transferee. The transferee argued that they were not entitled to receive compensation for unfair dismissal or a redundancy payment as they had only been employed with the transferee for 11 months. The court held that the employees' claim succeeded. Since the employees had negotiated continuation of their employment they had clearly not 'objected' to the transfer within the meaning of reg. 5(4A). Even though the employees had signed a form agreeing to opt out of the transfer, they had not, in fact, objected to the transfer and their employment was seamless. The question of whether the employees objected to the transfer was one of fact for the employment tribunal to decide. Their employment was also continuous under the TUPE regulations. The payment of a redundancy payment did not break continuity as there had been no dismissal. There would therefore be no set off between the redundancy and severance previously received against that which was due on termination of their employment.

5.15 TRANSFER IS SIGNIFICANT AND TO THE EMPLOYEE'S DETRIMENT

This clause reads as follows:

> Paragraphs (1) and (4A) above are without prejudice to any right of employee arising apart from these Regulations to terminate his contract of employment without notice if a substantial change is made in his working conditions to his detriment; but no such right shall arise by reason only that under this paragraph, the identity of his employer changes unless the employee shows that, in all the circumstances, the change is a significant change and is to his detriment.

Under reg. 5(5) employees can resign and treat themselves as dismissed where substantial changes are made to their working conditions, to their detriment. This provision merely preserves the existing rights at common law (see *Western Excavating (EEC) Ltd v. Sharpe* [1978] IRLR 27, [1978] ICR 221, CA). Employees cannot claim constructive dismissal against the transferee unless they are employed by the transferee. If an employee leaves before the transfer, in anticipation of the breach, there will be no remedy against the transferee for repudiatory breach (*Sita (GB) Ltd v. Burton* [1997] IRLR 501, EAT). This case also held that a proposed breach by the transferee does not constitute a breach of the transferee's duty not to undermine trust and confidence in the employment relationship, where there is a significant change in the identity of the employer and the change in that identity is to the employee's detriment and as a result the employee resigns.

The crucial question here is to determine when the change relates to the identity of the employer and when it is significant. It is unlikely that alterations in non-contractual terms and conditions or pension rights will be deemed significant. Terms and conditions of employment do not relate to the identity of the employer. The complaint must be that the objection relates to the actual identity of the employer.

Two recent cases have discussed this clause and have considered its effect and its interrelationship with reg. 5(4A) and 5(4B). Regulation 5 merely confirms that an employee shall retain the common law right to claim constructive dismissal against a transferor in respect of breaches (and anticipatory breaches) of contract.

In *University of Oxford* v. *Humphreys and the AEB* [2000] IRLR 183, CA Mr Humphreys was employed by Oxford University as a deputy examinations officer. His contract was to continue until retiring age unless terminated for misconduct or disobedience. In 1995 the university announced its intention of transferring the examining unit to the AEB. Mr Humphreys notified the university that he was exercising his right under TUPE reg. 5(4)A to object to being employed by the transferee, as this would have involved a significant change in his working conditions to his detriment, as a result in the change of identity of the employer.

In March 1995 the transfer took place and Mr Humphreys brought an action against the university claiming constructive dismissal on the basis of its anticipatory breach. It was conceded that the transfer to the AEB would involve a substantial change in Mr Humphreys's working conditions which would also be to his detriment. The university relied upon reg. 5(4B) saying that the employee had objected to the transfer and therefore could not claim constructive dismissal against it. It further argued that if such a claim could be bought then it should pass to the transferee, the AEB.

The Court of Appeal held that the common law right to claim constructive dismissal was preserved by reg. 5(5) which had to be interpreted as overriding reg. 5(4B). On the second matter, it was held that liability for wrongful dismissal did not transfer on the basis that it was a common law remedy and existed only in relation to the dismissing employer. The court also confirmed that reg. 5(5) could apply to an anticipatory breach.

Regulation 5(5) does not have to be read in conjunction with reg. 5(4B), but reg. 5(5) must be read purposively and overrides reg. 5(4B). This construction is in accordance with art. 4(2) of the Directive and the case of *Merckx* v. *Ford Company Motors Belgium SA* [1996] IRLR 467, ECJ, where it was said that if the terms of engagement of the transferee would be significantly different from those of the transferor and the difference would be detrimental to the employee then the employee had the option of treating the employment as terminated and obtaining compensation. The employee's rights would be against the transferor, not against the transferee, as the employment contract itself did not transfer across.

We have now seen this argument developed in the case of *Rossiter* v. *Pendragon plc* (CA, 10 May 2002). Mr Rossiter was employed by Lexford as a cars sales executive. In October 1997 Pendragon Motor Group acquired Lexford in a relevant transfer. On 15 February 1999 Mr Rossiter resigned from Pendragon on the grounds that his position had become untenable in that he had been constructively dismissed by the company because of the termination of his employment was by reason of his substantial change in his working conditions to his detriment within the provisions of TUPE reg. 5(5). These detrimental changes were:

(a) alterations in the way commission was calculated;
(b) that holiday pay would no longer be based on annual commission; and
(c) the erosion of his duties and responsibilities.

Mr Rossiter also pleaded that his dismissal was by reason of the transfer and, therefore, automatically unfair under reg. 8(1).

The EAT found that the combined effect of the Directive, TUPE regulations and the Employment Rights Act 1996 meant in the context of TUPE a substantial change in the employee's working conditions to his detriment was sufficient to amount to a 'constructive dismissal' regardless of whether that involved a fundamental breach. This was a right under TUPE reg. 5(5) and of a purposive interpretation of the Directive in that the Directive applied not only to contractual terms but also in the wider context.

This then went to the Court of Appeal where it was confirmed that a change to an employee's terms and conditions of employment for a transfer to which TUPE applies does not automatically amount to a constructive dismissal. An employee will still need to show a fundamental breach of his contractual rights. A transferee can, therefore, vary the terms and conditions of employment if a change would *not* amount to a fundamental breach. It was confirmed that no new right was created by reg. 5(5), only conduct amounting to a repudiation by an employer would entitle the employee to terminate a contract without notice. The EAT had erred in holding that the Employment Rights Act 1996, s.95(1)(c) should be construed in a way that enables an employee to claim constructive dismissal where there was no repudiatory breach. The test in *Western Excavating (ECC) Ltd* v. *Sharpe* [1978] QB 761 applied to both situations where there was a transfer and where there was no transfer. There is no guidance as to what 'significant' means – it could mean 'other than nominal'. The word detriment also bears some resemblance to the language of discrimination law and could relate to the known conduct of the employer with regard to any of the following:

• equal opportunities practices;
• union recognition;
• health and safety;
• poor industrial relations.

It could also relate to wider issues such as environmental transgressions or political views of the board of directors. The courts have, however, not yet tested these words.

5.16 WRITTEN TERMS OF EMPLOYMENT

The transferee is not required to provide employees with a fresh statement of terms and conditions of employment under the Employment Rights Act 1996, s.1. Only an amendment need be provided under s.4 of the Act, notifying a change in the identity of the employer (see Appendix 5, letters nos. 6 and 7).

5.17 ADVICE AT THE TRANSFER STAGE

Advising the transferor

At this stage of a transfer, the transferor will already have complied with the duty to inform and consult. The next stage that the transferor should address is identifying which employees will be affected by the transfer. This will include those who are not employed in the part transferred but will be in some way affected by the transfer itself. The transferor also has to identify which employees will be working in the part transferred and who will actually transfer with the undertaking. The transferor will have to establish the following facts with regard to those being employed in the part transferred:

(a) the rights that the employees will transfer with;
(b) which employees object to the transfer.

The transferor will also have to advise employees of the facts of the transfer. The transferor should also consider telling employees who objected to the transfer the effect that this has upon their employment law rights, as an objection would be an unreserved resignation and the employee would not transfer (1.8).

In the weeks leading up to the transfer, the transferor should be advised to draw up a schedule of all those employed immediately before the transfer, or reasonably proximate to it. The transferor should be advised not to dismiss or allow the transferee to dismiss any employees close to the transfer, as if the dismissals were deemed to be for a reason relating to the transfer, they would be deemed to be automatically unfair. This would not prevent the transferor dismissing for a reason that was in no way connected to the transfer, e.g. for misconduct or retirement or for ill health, but caution should be advised. The transferor should also be advised to discuss with any employees who are absent on account of long-term sickness whether they wish to seek ill health retirement and draw a pension. Since the case of *Bernadone* it is clear that employees will transfer with the benefit of any insurance cover that may be in place. However, pension rights do not transfer, unless the benefit in the pension scheme does not relate to retirement benefits as seen in the case of *Beckmann* v. *Dynamco Whicheloe Macfarlane Ltd* (C-16/00) (ECJ, June 2002).

If the transferor decides to dismiss any employees close to the date of the transfer, it should disclose this to the transferee as the latter may become liable to face a claim for unfair dismissal or breach of contract.

The transferor should therefore provide the following information to the transferee:

(a) details of all employees transferring to the transferee. However, the Data Protection Act 1998 should be taken into account before the files are transferred to the transferee. If any employees do not transfer, the files should be handed back to the transferor or destroyed (or perhaps sent to the employee if the Transferor will cease to exist after the transfer);

(b) details of all contractual rights and obligations of those transferring, including the details of any collective agreements that apply;

(c) details of any outstanding claims that any transferring employees may have against the transferor in respect of breach of contract, breaches of race, sex, disability and part time discrimination legislation and breaches of the working time regulations. Details should also be provided of any outstanding disciplinary sanctions outstanding on employee's files as well as any grievance procedures that may be pending;

(d) details of any dismissals that have been carried out by the transferor within three months of the date of the transfer, giving the reason for the dismissal and the length of service of the employee, the earnings of the employee and the effective date of termination;

(e) details of all the consultation that has taken place with the employees and the information that was provided to the employees upon which to consult;

(f) copies of any compromise agreements signed by employees who have pursued a negotiated settlement or accepted a voluntary redundancy settlement as a result of the transfer (if any).

If the transferor is requested by the transferee to provide copies of personnel files, it is essential to consider withholding information which is confidential or sensitive or a breach of the right to privacy which could be a breach of the Data Protection Act 1998 or the Human Rights Act 1998. If any employees object to the transfer and letters should be sent advising them of the consequences of their objecting to the transfer. Then, if they still wish to object, request that they sign a letter to the transferor confirming that they object to the transfer.

Near to the time of the transfer it is advisable for a transferor to write to all employees who are transferring to inform them that the transfer is to take place and the effect that the transfer will have on their contracts of employment. A suggested form of a letter appears as letter no. 6 at Appendix 5.

Advising the transferee

A transferee should be encouraged to ask searching questions about actions that have been taken by the transferor in connection with the workforce. If possible, all the staff movements should be established in order that the full potential liability of any possible claims can be assessed. Questions should be asked about the status of all workers, including agency and part-time workers, irrespective of the number of hours worked and the type of contracts that they are serving under.

The questions that the transferee must ask the transferor concern:

(a) the provision of full details (ages, pay, length of service, titles, holiday entitlement, parental leave taken, covenants, etc.) for all employees, contractors, agency staff and casual workers who are due to transfer, including the details of those who would have transferred had they not been dismissed reasonably proximate to the transfer;

(b) the indemnities required from the transferor in respect of any employee recently dismissed or in respect of other claims that are pending upon transfer (see Appendix 6);

(c) full details of the consultations conducted by the transferee with the employees who will transfer prior to the transfer taking place as well as consultation with its own employees who may be affected by the transfer;

(d) which of the transferor's employees have opted to take a voluntary severance payment rather than to transfer to the transferee. The transferee must ensure that these employees are not taken on as the employees may retain continuity of service if they are paid a contractual redundancy payment and then taken on by the transferee. It is only a statutory redundancy payment that breaks continuity of service, therefore, voluntary severance terms will not prevent continuous service accruing.

The transferee should then ensure that an amendment to the employees' contracts is issued giving the details of the new employer and affirming that all contractual terms remain the same. No other changes should be made to the contract without the express written consent of the parties (see draft letter no. 7 at Appendix 5).

No changes in the transferred employees' terms or to other employees' terms and conditions of employment should be made unless the transferee can avail itself of an ETO defence (see Chapter 6).

Advising the employee

When advising employees, it is essential to establish whether they are happy with the concept of transferring across to the transferee or whether they have fundamental objections to working for it. If they have any such objections, they can refuse to transfer but in doing so, they would be dismissing themselves and would have no claim against either the transferor or the transferee. If employees have a fundamental objection to working for the transferee because this would result in a significant change to their working conditions to their detriment, employees can resign and claim constructive dismissal against the transferor. This would only be a viable prospect if the transferor were solvent, as the claim is against the transferor alone.

Most employees seeking legal advice in connection with a transfer will be seeking reassurance as to their legal rights and any rights to receive a severance payment, if redundancy were offered as an alternative to transferring.

When providing advice to employees it is essential to obtain as much information about the transfer as possible. This may not always be easy as many transfers may take place under a cloak of secrecy and few if any details may be available until the last minute. The way in which advice is to be structured should be as follows:

1. Advise on whether the TUPE regulations apply and give as much advice as possible about the circumstances under which they have been held to apply in the past. Try to apply the case law on what constitutes to a transfer to the facts known about the particular case.

2. Establish the extent of the employee's contractual and statutory rights by obtaining a copy of the employees' contract, staff handbook, collective agreements, etc. Assess the rights that the employee will transfer across with (if transferred).

3. Take instructions as to the proposals before the employee that are being made in connection with the transfer. Advise the employee as to the full effects of the TUPE regulations and then establish the best route for the employee to take. Consider all of the following:

   (a) offers of redundancy/early retirement with an enhanced pension;

   (b) length of service of the employee and the opportunities with the transferee company and the value of these rights to the employee as opposed to the opportunities with any other company where employment protection rights would be lost;

   (c) contractual restrictions placed upon the employee by the contract and any compromise agreement that may be proposed, when advising the employee as to opportunities outside the transferee company;

   (d) anticipatory breaches in the employment contract arising in connection with the transfer. These could include changes in the geographical location of the place of work (if the employment contract does not contain a mobility clause), changes in hierarchy, changes in job description and status. If it looks likely that breaches will occur, the employee must be advised of his or her right to claim for unfair and constructive dismissal against either the transferor or the transferee and the effect of the employer's defence of an ETO (see Chapter 6) in respect of those changes.

4. Advise the employees that his or her employment contract will transfer across to the transferee on the same terms and conditions (apart from occupational pension rights). In addition to the contractual rights transferring, the employee will transfer with the following rights against the transferee:

   (a) the right to retain continuity of employment;
   (b) the right to claim for discrimination in respect of acts that occurred before the transfer;
   (c) the right to payment under profit sharing schemes in respect of the 'profit year' in respect of when the transfer took effect;
   (d) the right not be dismissed for a reason connected to the transfer;
   (e) the right to bring a tortious claim in respect of personal injury sustained while in the transferor's employment;
   (f) the right to bring a claim for negligent misstatement against the transferee in respect of misrepresentations made by the transferor before the transfer.

If the employee is likely to wish to pursue any of the above claims, it would be prudent to advise the employee to inform the transferee of the existence of these rights shortly after the transfer and to lodge proceedings in accordance with the respective time limits. These prospective claims will obviously transfer across to the transferee (if reg. 5 applies) but, if the claim is under discrimination legislation (race, sex, disability or part-time status) in respect of a continuing act, the transfer may break the chain of causation of the continuing act (i.e. by moving the employee away from a team of discriminators). If that is the case then the employee must lodge any claim within three months of the transfer in order to protect the claim. The employee should also be advised as to the law on victimisation, in case the transferee decides to take retributive action against the employee for lodging a claim in order to protect his or her interests on transfer.

Claims in respect of failure to inform and consult do not transfer to the transferee. Also the transferee does not assume a liability for negligent misrepresentations made in respect of pension rights as the pension rights themselves do not transfer under reg. 7.

CHAPTER 6
Dismissals

6.1 LEGISLATIVE PROVISIONS

The objective of the Directive and the regulations

The overriding purpose of the Directive 2001/23/EC (the Directive) is to provide for the protection of employees in the event of a change of employer, and in particular to ensure that their rights are safeguarded. The TUPE regulations attempt to do this by providing that employees have the right to be informed and consulted before a transfer and, if employees so choose, they have a right to work for the transferee on their same terms and conditions of employment that they enjoyed with the transferor with recognition of their continuous service. The only terms that do not transfer are pension rights (reg. 7); see *Walden Engineering Co. Ltd* v. *Warrener* [1993] IRLR 420, EAT (see 7.2).

Who has the protection of the TUPE regulations?

Under art. 2 (2) of the Directive, member states are allowed to extend the rights contained in the Directive only to those employees who have the protection of employment law status under their particular national jurisdiction. It is stated in art. 4 of the Directive that:

> The transfer of an Undertaking, business or part of a business shall not itself constitute grounds for dismissal by the Transferor or the Transferee. This provision shall not stand in the way of dismissals that may take place for an economic, technical or organisational reason entailing changes in the workforce.
>
> Member States may provide that the [above] shall not apply to certain specific categories of employees who are not covered by the laws and practice of Member States in respect of protection against dismissal.

The Directive makes it clear that member states should not exclude part-time or temporary employees or those who are employed under a fixed term contract from the provisions of their domestic regulations. The only employees or workers who therefore may not enjoy the protection rights under TUPE reg. 8 are:

(a) employees with less than one year's service, as they do not presently have employment protection rights in respect of unfair dismissal in the Employment Rights Act 1996;

(b) agency workers (but see *Motorola* v. *Davidson* and *Melville Craig Group Limited* [2001] IRLR 4 at 2.1);

(c) casual workers as defined in the case of *Carmichael* v. *National Power* (see 2.1);

(d) genuinely independent contractors (but see *Reid* v. *North West Ceilings Limited T/A Shopspec* (EAT, 2 April 2001) at 2.1).

All other classes of employees and workers have a right to pursue a claim to assert their employment law rights under TUPE. The regulations give no additional rights to employees, they only protect the legal rights and interests of employees that exist at the date of the transfer.

Rights under TUPE regulation 8

Under reg. 8, an employee is protected from a dismissal which is for a reason, or principal reason, which is connected with the transfer, by making such a dismissal automatically unfair.

Regulation 8 states:

> where either before or after a relevant transfer, any employee of the transferor or transferee is dismissed, that employee shall be treated . . . as unfairly dismissed if the transfer or a reason connected with it is the principal reason for his dismissal . . .

Regulation 8(2) provides the employer with a defence to a claim for automatically unfair dismissal lodged by an employee. The defence states:

> Where an economic technical or organisational reason entailing changes in the workforce of either the transferor or the transferee before or after the relevant transfer is the reason or principal reason for dismissing an employee
>
> (a) paragraph (1) above shall not apply to his dismissal;
> (b) . . . the dismissal shall . . . be regarded as having been for a substantial reason of a kind as to justify the dismissal of an employee holding the position which the employee held.

Regulation 8(3) states that 'the provisions of this Regulation apply whether or not the employee in question is employed in the undertaking or part of the undertaking transferred or to be transferred'. Where a reason is found to fall within reg. 8(2) it constitutes a substantial reason which is capable of justifying a dismissal within the meaning of s.98(1)(b) of the Employment Rights Act 1996. In such a case the dismissal will not be automatically unfair but it may still be unfair by virtue of an infringement of s.98(4) of the Employment Rights Act 1996. Even where the dismissing employer has a valid ETO defence, that defence is only capable of unseating the presumption that the dismissal is automatically unfair, as stated in reg. 8(1). The dismissal will then be subjected to scrutiny by the employment tribunal to see whether the dismissal was fair and in accordance with the principles set out in s.98(4), which states that:

> Where the employer has fulfilled the requirements of subsection (1), the determination of the question whether the dismissal is fair or unfair (having regard to the reason shown by the employer)
>
> (a) depends upon whether in the circumstances (including the size and administrative resources of the employers undertaking) the employer acted reasonably or unreasonably in treating it as a sufficient reason for dismissing the employee and
> (b) should be determined in accordance with equity and the substantial merits of the case.

In order for the employer to show that the dismissal was fair, it has to be shown that it was procedurally and substantively fair. The only way that this can conclusively be shown to the tribunal is by having evidence of good information and consultation procedures with documented and minuted meetings. Fair procedures must also be followed when moving to dismissal, including the right for an employee to know the reason for dismissal with a hearing against nomination for dismissal and an appeal against the dismissal. The employee must also be allowed the right to be accompanied by a representative to all hearings that may lead to dismissal (this will often be the appropriate representative under the Employment Relations Act 1999). Most employees who are dismissed as a result of a relevant transfer will be dismissed by reason of redundancy or reorganisation, and it will be important to establish objective criteria for nominating employees for redundancy. Those criteria must not be tainted by any directly or indirectly discriminatory intentions, for example using part-time status or length of service as a criterion may be direct discrimination and contrary to the Part Time Workers Regulations or it could be indirect discrimination contrary to the Sex Discrimination Act 1975.

6.2 REASON CONNECTED WITH THE TRANSFER

If a dismissal takes place for a reason connected with the transfer and an employee is dismissed, either before the transfer by the transferor or after the transfer by the transferee, such a dismissal may be held to be automatically unfair. If a dismissed employee lodges proceedings under reg. 8 and can show that there was a causal connection between the relevant transfer and the dismissal, it will be for the dismissing employer to show that:

(a) it was not for a reason connected with the transfer and therefore not automatically unfair and

(b) it was for a fair reason within the Employment Rights Act 1996, s.98(4).

It will be a matter of evidence as to whether the dismissal was deemed to be by reason of the transfer. Obviously, the greater the length of time between the dismissal and the date of the transfer, the easier it may be to displace the inference that a dismissal was by reason of the transfer.

Even where a dismissal takes place at a time which is reasonably proximate to the time of the transfer, this does not mean that it will always be held to be automatically unfair. If there is a legitimate reason to dismiss an employee for one of the five fair reasons to dismiss under the Employment Rights Act 1996, s.98, and that reason is not in any way connected with the transfer, that dismissal will not become automatically unfair because of the proximity of the transfer.

It is important to remember that employees transfer to the transferee with all existing rights and liabilities. Therefore, if an employee transfers to the transferee with a final warning on the file, the fact that the employee commits a final act of misconduct the day after the transfer will not make any subsequent dismissal of that employee automatically unfair under reg. 8 as the dismissal would not be related in any way to the transfer; there would be a fair reason to dismiss on conduct alone. However, it is for the dismissing employer to show that the dismissal was in no way connected with the transfer and that it was for a fair reason. As with all claims for unfair dismissal, the dismissing employer can only put forward a good defence if fair procedures are followed, and this will include allowing a hearing and an appeal against dismissal, as this will soon become a statutory obligation when the Employment Act 2002 comes into force in April 2003. It is prudent to ensure that all procedural safeguards are in place to show to the court (or tribunal) that the dismissal was both procedurally and substantively fair and not related in any way to the transfer. The precise reason for the dismissal must be carefully documented after the hearing and the appeal has taken place and after all representations have been taken into account.

6.3 IMMINENT TRANSFER?

A question has arisen as to whether a dismissal will be automatically unfair if it is by reason of a *particular* transfer or whether it is enough that a transfer will take place to some transferee even though there is no specific transferee in mind. The use of the words 'by reason of *the* transfer' in reg. 8(2) would appear to mean that there has to be a specific transfer in mind. The case of *Harrison Bowden Ltd* v. *Bowden* [1994] ICR 186, EAT supported the view that reg. 8 would apply to any transfer, even if the identity of the transferee were not known at the time. However, in *Ibex Trading Co. Ltd* v. *Walton* [1994] IRLR 564 the EAT took a more restrictive view and the court held that notice should be taken of the definite article and therefore the TUPE regulations could not apply where dismissals took effect before a transferee was identified. *Michael Peters Ltd* v. *Farnfield and Michael Peters Group plc* [1995] IRLR 190 followed *Bowden* and held that the definite article in reg. 8 was of no great significance.

In *Morris* v. *John Grose Group Ltd* [1998] IRLR 499 the EAT also went back to the broad brush approach adopted in *Bowden* case and said that the *Ibex* case had been wrongly decided. Here receivers decided to make redundancies three days before speaking to a purchaser of the business. The decision to make the redundancies was taken with a view to increasing the prospects of selling the business as a going concern. It was therefore held that the dismissals were connected for a reason relating to the transfer was even though the sale took place five weeks later. *Morris* confirms that any dismissal in contemplation of a transfer may be found to be in breach of reg. 8 and therefore automatically unfair even if the identity of the transferee is not known at the time of the dismissal.

Whether a dismissal is connected with a transfer would be proved by evidence. Where a transfer is reasonably proximate in time to the transfer an inference can be drawn that the dismissal was connected with the transfer. The burden of proof is on the employer to show that the connection does not exist. The longer the gap between the dismissal and the transfer the easier, evidentially, the employer's job will be in proving that the dismissal is not connected with the transfer. But a gap will not always save the employer, as was seen in the case of *Allen* v. *Amalgamated Construction Co. Ltd* [2000] IRLR 119, ECJ (see above), when the break of a weekend did not prevent the TUPE regulations from applying to post-dismissal re-engagement, entitling the employees to claim continuity of service and the benefit of their old contracts.

6.4 REMEDIES AVAILABLE

It is clear from reg. 8 that the only remedy available to an employee is the remedy of unfair dismissal. In the case of *Betts* v. *Brintel Helicopters Ltd and KLM ERA Helicopters (UK) Ltd* [1997] IRLR 361 the court held that since it had no jurisdiction to restrain by injunction the dismissal of the plaintiffs (as the dismissal was not connected with the transfer), the remedy lay exclusively within unfair dismissal law. There is also the possibility that an employee could claim for breach of contract in respect of a breach of the implied term of trust and confidence.

6.5 LIABILITY FOR DISMISSAL

The normal principle of law is that the person dismissing is liable for legal consequences of the dismissal. The case of *Litster* held that if the dismissal was by reason of the transfer and but for the dismissal the employee would have been employed in the part of the under-taking transferred, the employee would automatically have trans-ferred under TUPE and any liability would pass to the transferee. The transferee steps into the shoes of the transferor for all purposes, including the payment of compensation for unfair dismissal.

If the transferor has entered into compromise agreements on all of the employee's claims, the transferee has the benefit of those agreements, if they were validly drafted and signed in accordance with the Employment Rights Act 1996, s.203(3). Some doubt has been expressed as to whether a compromise agreement used in con-nection with a dismissal by reason of a transfer would be deemed to be void under reg. 12, as an attempt to contract out of the rights under the TUPE regulations. It is now accepted that any acts done by the transferor, prior to the transfer, are deemed to be done by the transferee. A compromise agreement signed by the employee and the transferor could be relied upon by the transferee. However, the principle will not assist a transferee if the compromise agreement with the transferor was effected after the date of the transfer, as was held in the case of *Thompson* v. *Walon Car Delivery and BRS Automotive Ltd* [1997] IRLR 343.

The transferee will not be responsible for all dismissals effected by reason of the transfer. Regulation 8 makes all dismissals automatically unfair, if they take place for a reason that is connected with a transfer, whether or not those dismissed are employed in the part of the undertaking transferred (see reg. 8(3)). However, liability only transfers to the transferee under reg. 5 in respect of persons employed by the transferor at the time of the transfer of the undertaking or part transferred (or would have been so employed if they had not been dismissed unfairly, as in *Litster*). The scope of reg. 5 is therefore narrower than reg. 8.

6.6 RETENDERING EXERCISES

Where an undertaking is transferred between contractors (after a retendering exercise), it was held in *Dines* v. *Initial Healthcare Services* and *Dines* v. *Pall Mall Services Group Ltd* [1994] IRLR 336, [1995] ICR 11, CA that in such situations there are two transfers: the original contractor transfers the business to the tendering company and then the tendering company transfers the business to the new contractor. The tendering company is the transferee of the first transaction and the transferor of the second. If the original contractor dismissed employees then there may be two possible outcomes, which are:

(a) if the dismissal is a nullity, the employees will pass to the new contractor and any failure to employ them will amount to a dismissal under reg. 8 (this point has now been resolved in the case of *Wilson* v. *St Helens* below); or

(b) the court may look at the two transactions as separate, effecting a transfer between one contractor and another.

6.7 PERSON EMPLOYED IN THE PART TRANSFERRED

Difficulties arise when only part of an undertaking is transferred. In the case of *Botzen* v. *Rotterdamsche Droogdok Maatschappij BV*

[1986] 2 CMLR 50, ECJ it was held that under European law the employees who transferred would be those who were allocated or assigned to the part transferred. The court adopted a pragmatic approach and found that the employee would have to work the whole of his time in the part transferred. The ECJ did not, however, adopt this test and but a looser one. In order to be held to be assigned to the part transferred, an employee only has to work for a *significant* amount of time in the part transferred. A range of considerations must be taken into account when deciding whether an employee is taken to be employed in the part transferred (see 5.3).

6.8   THE EFFECT OF A DISMISSAL

There has been much legal debate as to whether the dismissal in connection with a transfer is either:

(a)   effective but automatically unfair; or
(b)   a nullity.

This situation has now been resolved by the case of *Wilson* v. *St Helens Borough Council* [1998] IRLR 706. Here it was held that the TUPE regulations do not require the dismissals to be treated as a nullity. The dismissal is effective to prevent the employee from later bringing a claim for deductions from wages because their delay in lodging proceedings amounted to an acquiescence to the new terms.

This case appears run counter to the earlier ECJ decision in *P. Bork International A/S* v. *Foreningen af Arbejdsledere i Danmark* (C-101/87) [1989] IRLR 41 in which the ECJ accepted the argument of the Commission that a transfer-related dismissal should be treated as ineffective in particular circumstances where the employee is taken on by the transferee after being dismissed by the transferor before the transfer, and he then seeks to assert his rights under art. 3 of the Directive. Any employee dismissed upon transfer and then subsequently re-engaged by the transferee should bring a claim for unfair dismissal against the transferee using reg. 5 if he or she wishes to be employed on previous terms and conditions by asking for a remedy of reinstatement or re-engagement. This would be adopting a purposive view of the Directive in order to enable employees to continue working in the transferred undertaking on the same terms and conditions as those for the transferor.

6.9 TUPE REGULATION 8(2)

A dismissal may be regarded as substantively fair if the employer can show it is for an ETO of either the transferor or the transferee, before or after the relevant transfer. The onus is on the employer to prove this.

The language of TUPE reg. 8(2) (see p.169) is lifted straight from the Directive. In the case of *D'Urso* v. *Ercole Marelli Elettromeccanica Generale SpA* [1992] IRLR 136 the Advocate General gave the wording a narrow interpretation. The view was expressed that the exception applied only if the dismissal would in any event have been effected by the transferor even if no transfer had occurred. It was the ECJ view in this case that it would be inconsistent with the objectives of the Directive to deprive any employees of rights recognised by the Directive when an undertaking was transferred. This construction has not been followed since.

The construction of reg. 8(2) is that the onus of proving an ETO lies on the employer. It is the employer which dismisses that must give the reason, even if it dismisses at the behest of the transferee. In *BSG Property Services* v. *Tuck* [1996] IRLR 134, EAT both the transferor and transferee were of the view that the TUPE regulations did not apply. The transferee told the transferor that it would not need any employees but did not ask the transferor to dismiss any. The transferee never had any reason to dismiss the employees, as it did not think it was taking on responsibility for them. In this case the transferor could not rely upon the transferee's ETO reasons. This case is probably distinguishable easily on its facts, since if the transferee had asked the transferor to make employees redundant because it had enough spare capacity, the transferor would have dismissed the employees on that ground.

In order to benefit from the defence contained in reg. 8(2) the ETO relied upon by the dismissing employer must relate to the conduct of the business and not merely be a reason designed to effect a sale or enhance the value of the business. *Whitehouse* v. *Blatchford & Sons Ltd* [1999] IRLR 492, CA involved outsourcing of a contract of prosthetic services to B Ltd. The hospital made it clear that the service was to be provided by 12 employees. The business had 13 employees at the time of the transfer. After the transfer B Ltd had no alternative but to dismiss one employee. The Court of Appeal held that this was a valid ETO as B Ltd would not have won the contract had it not agreed to this provision. In this case it was held that the word 'economic' was to have the same meaning as 'technical and organisational', meaning that the reason must be concerned with the actual running of the business. A dismissal in order to achieve a sale or to make the business more attractive to a purchaser was not regarded as having anything to do with the day to day conduct of the business. (In this case the dismissal was at the behest of the transferee which refused to proceed with the sale unless the employees were dismissed.)

Genuine redundancies or the need to make redundancies can constitute an 'economic' reason, provided that staff are not engaged under different terms or others are not hired to replace them. In the case of *Bork* (see above) the ECJ held that the fact that employees had been re-engaged by the transferee would exclude a finding that the dismissal had been for an ETO. Just because a dismissal is for redundancy within a transfer situation does not prevent it from being within reg. 8(2). If it were a genuine redundancy then the employee would be entitled to a redundancy payment (see *Gorictree Ltd* v. *Jenkinson* [1984] IRLR 391, EAT).

The case of *Thompson* v. *SCS Consulting Limited* [2001] IRLR 801, EAT found that receivers who dismissed 25 employees 11 hours before the transfer dismissed the employees for an ETO; the reason given was that they were 'not required for the operation of the business and it would not be economically viable for the business to continue if the dismissed employees remained in the employ of the vendors'. As the dismissals related to the conduct of the business this was a valid ETO.

'Technical' will cover situations when new machinery or methods of working are introduced and/or where the existing employees may not have the appropriate skills. 'Organisational' reasons include situations such as where the transferee decides to integrate its newly acquired workforce with its existing workforce so that fewer people are needed to do the job. It could also cover situations where the transferee decides to supply the services in a different way. This could be illustrated by the case of *Porter* v. *Queens Medical Centre* [1993] IRLR 486. In a contracting out situation services were reorganised. The applicants' posts were disbanded and four posts were created which required specialised knowledge that the applicants did not have. The applicants were interviewed for the positions but were unsuccessful. They were therefore dismissed by reason of an organisational change in the workforce.

6.10 ETO TEST

The ETO is a two-stage test. First it has to be proved by the employer that the dismissal was for an economic, technical or organisational reason and secondly that this reason 'entailed a change in the workforce'. The employer's plan must be to achieve changes in the workforce. It must be an objective of the plan and not merely a consequence. 'Changes in the workforce' mean a change in the number or function of the workforce not changes in their financial working conditions. This was the decision of *Berriman* v. *Delabole Slate Ltd* [1985] ICR 546 where the transferee sought to reduce the applicant's pay, so that he had the same terms and conditions as all other staff. He therefore claimed constructive dismissal. The Court of Appeal held that the reason for the change was an economic reason, but the case fell down on the second limb of the test in that it did not entail changes in the workforce. The transferee needed the same number of employees but wanted them on standardised terms and conditions. It was held that the change of employees working on different terms and conditions did not constitute a change in the workforce. A workforce was a body of employees working in the business. A change in the identity of those persons did not constitute a change in the workforce where there was no accompanying material change in the function or numbers.

In the case of *Crawford* v. *Swinton Insurance Brokers Ltd* [1990] IRLR 42, EAT it was held that there may be changes in the workforce if the functions performed by the employees change even if the numbers and identities of the staff stay the same. However, compare this with that of *Wilson* v. *St Helens Borough Council* [1998] IRLR 706, HL, where it was held that the dismissals of staff fell within reg. 8(2) even though many of the employees had to be retained on different terms and conditions of employment. It may be that this case was decided on its facts alone, the court taking into account the fact that the employees worked on without challenge for one year after the contractual changes were imposed. The decision of Lord Slynn is particularly useful in this case.

6.11 POTENTIALLY FAIR DISMISSALS

There are conflicting views as to whether a dismissal will transfer across to the transferee when it is not automatically unfair as in reg. 8(2) where a dismissal for an ETO may make such a dismissal fair. Such dismissals can be valid, fair and effective in bringing the contract to an end. Where a dismissal is found to be for an ETO under reg. 8(2), reg. 8(1) no longer applies and the liability for the dismissal will not transfer to the transferee. The onus is on the dismissing employer to establish that the reason for the dismissal is an ETO (*Gateway Hotels Ltd* v. *Stewart* [1988] IRLR 287, EAT).

It has been submitted in the case of *Litster* that liability for such dismissals does not transfer to the transferee. The reasoning behind this logic is that reg. 8(2) dismissals are capable of being lawful and binding. If, however, the decision to dismiss has been unlawfully implemented liability *could* transfer to the transferee. This has now been confirmed in the case of *Thompson* v. *SCS Consulting Ltd and Others* (EAT, 3 September 2001). In this case it was held that the dismissing employer, who was the transferor, had an effective ETO (which was that the business was overstaffed and inefficient and could only be made viable and sold off to the transferee if the workforce was reduced). The dismissals were therefore not automatically unfair under reg. 8(1). This view adopted the purposive construction to the words 'immediately before the transfer'; therefore *Litster* did not apply as the employees had been dismissed 11 hours earlier so that reg. 5 did not operate to transfer the rights or liabilities. The only remedy was against the transferor because the dismissal was for an ETO. Even though the dismissals were at the instance of the transferee, liability for the dismissal did not pass to the transferee, even though they were found to be unfair.

In *Litster* the relationship between reg. 8(1) and reg. 8(2) was considered. It was held in a previous unreported case of *Honeycombe 78 Ltd* v. *Cummings* (EAT/100/99) that if the transferee can show that the transferor's reason, or principal reason, for the dismissal was an ETO, then reg. 8(1) is displaced, even if the dismissal is considered to be unfair. The question of the reason for the dismissal is one of fact for the tribunal. The EAT summarised the principles as follows:

1. If reg. 8(2) applies, reg. 8(1) is excluded and the extended construction of reg. 5(3) in *Litster* does not apply. If the tribunal concludes that the reason or principal reason was the transfer, reg. 8(2) does not apply, the *Litster* principle does or may apply and the dismissals are automatically unfair (as in the cases of *Litster* and *Whitehouse* v. *Blatchford* below).

2. In deciding whether an ETO reason was or was not the reason or the principal reason for the dismissal, the tribunal is making

a factual decision (as in the *Whitehouse* v. *Blatchford* and *Kerry Foods* cases).

3. In making that factual decision, the tribunal must consider whether the reason was connected with the future conduct of the business as a going concern (as in the cases of *Wheeler* and *Whitehouse* v. *Blatchford*).

4. The tribunal is entitled to take into account as relevant factual material, whether there was any collusion between the transferor and the transferee and whether the transferor or those acting on its behalf had any funds to carry on the business or any business at the time of the decision to dismiss (as in the cases of *Spence* and *Litster*).

5. An appellate tribunal should only interfere with a factual decision if the tribunal erred in law by applying the wrong test, by considering an irrelevant factor, by failing to consider a relevant factor or by reaching a perverse decision.

It is essential to ensure that a dismissal takes effect before the transfer by the transferor ensuring that notice of dismissal is delivered to the employee in person. Notice is not effective to terminate a contract of employment unless it is actually received by the employee. If the transferor fails to provide notice to the employee before the transfer, the employee's rights will transfer to the transferee in accordance with reg. 5.

6.12 CLAIMS TRANSFERRING WHEN A DISMISSAL TAKES PLACE BEFORE THE TRANSFER

Where a dismissal is effected by the transferor prior to the transfer, but for a reason connected with the transfer, the dismissal will be effective to terminate the contract even though the dismissal may be automatically unfair. The employee will have an enforceable claim against the transferee in respect of outstanding statutory rights as if he had been dismissed by the transferee. Those rights include:

(a) arrears of pay;

(b) notice pay in respect of statutory notice;

(c) any other statutory claims in respect of a failure to allow a right to representation under the Employment Relations Act 1999;

(d) holiday pay;

(e) redundancy pay (if the employee has been employed for two years or more);

(f) unfair dismissal compensation (if the employee was employed for one year or more) relating to procedural or substantive unfairness.;

(g) any other contractual entitlements not met by the transferor (including bonuses, commission and profit share schemes);

(h) any other claims subsisting at the date of termination against the transferor;

(i) any claims in respect of discrimination (sex, race, disability, equal pay, part-time status, gender reassignment).

6.13 TRANSFEROR'S RELIANCE ON TRANSFEREE'S ETO

Regulation 8(2) states that a reason may be that of the transferor or the transferee before or after the relevant transfer. This suggests that transferor can, before the transfer, rely on an ETO of the transferee, as long as it involves a change in the workforce. The transferor needs to be aware of the consequences of implementing such a dismissal. Those consequences are:

1. The transferor will have to demonstrate that it acted reasonably within ss.98(4)–(6) of the Employment Rights Act 1996. This means the transferor must consult and consider suitable alternative employment. It may be necessary to enquire of the transferee whether or not the reason for redundancy is a genuine reason.

2. If there is no reason under TUPE reg. 8(2) the reason will fall within reg. 8(1) and be automatically unfair.

3. If there is a reg. 8(2) dismissal, which is found to be unfair in all the circumstances of the case due to a breach of the Employment Rights Act 1996, s.98 it is likely that the liability for the unfair dismissal will remain with the transferor. Therefore, those acting for the transferor would be well advised to recommend that any dismissals carried out before the transfer be carried out procedurally and substantively fairly.

4. There is a benefit for the transferee in asking the transferor to make employees redundant. If the transferor selects a person for redundancy, the selection can only be made from the transferor's workplace and the transferee does not have to consider making any of its own employees redundant. If the transferee wishes to make employees redundant after the transfer and it selects only those transferred from the transferor's business the selection may be automatically unfair under reg. 8 as the dismissal will

clearly be for a reason connected with the transfer. It would then be for the transferee to show that it had an ETO.

6.14 HARMONISING TERMS AND CONDITIONS OF EMPLOYMENT

Where a transferee takes over an undertaking it will often seek to harmonise terms and conditions of employment. This may be for many different reasons – for example to reduce costs, or to bring them in line with those of other employers. If the transferee seeks to make these changes following a transfer and only because of the transfer itself, the changes and any resultant dismissals will be automatically unfair. The Court of Appeal in the case of *Berriman* v. *Delabole Slate* confirmed that upon any such contractual changes for reasons entailing a change in the workforce will render a decision automatically unfair. The court advised that in such cases, the employer would have to harmonise terms and conditions in accordance with the most favourable. In other words, it would have to bring all employees up to the better terms and conditions, which would usually be those of transferred employees, in order not to fall foul of the TUPE regulations, or to run the risk of complaints for breach of contract or for constructive unfair dismissal. The court held that that was what the TUPE regulations expected and this was again adopting a purposive approach.

The reasoning of the Court of Appeal in *Berriman* is as follows:

1. 'Entailing changes in the workforce' is a change in the 'strength' or 'establishment'. It does not mean changes in the contractual terms of the individuals who make up the workforce. Workforce means the whole body of employees as an entity.
2. Where constructive dismissal is argued, the reason for the dismissal is the employer's reason for breaching the contract.
3. Attempting to standardise or harmonise terms and conditions of employment does not bring about or entail a change in the workforce. There was only a possibility that this would happen if employees refused the change.
4. The 'possibility' was not sufficient to bring the reason within reg. 8(2) as the changes in the workforce must be the objective of the plan, not merely a consequence that might follow from its implementation

Harmonisation is always a major difficulty for a transferee employer. Non-financial changes to a contract (to include hours, place of work, etc.) are more likely to come within an ETO definition where there are organisational changes designed to bring people within a new working environment. To effect changes in financial terms and conditions of employment, the employer will still have to show that the employee is doing a substantially different job. It could also be argued that a benefit that was previously offered by the transferor could no longer be offered by the transferee because it related to benefits that could only be offered by the transferor. An example of this is where a discount card is offered to employees for companies within the group or where a profit-related bonus scheme is linked to the performance of a group of companies. When the transferor transfers one company out of the group to a transferee, the bonus may no longer be paid as it related to a historical calculation of the profits of another organisation. (However, see the case of *Mitie Managed Services Ltd* v. *French & others* (EAT, 12 April 2002) (409/00).)

There may be situations where the employee's job moves to a new location, which would allow the employer to pay less money, and indeed this may also be a redundancy situation (but the contract may have to be looked at to see if there is a mobility clause to cover the change in the physical work environment).

Changes can always be made to an employee's contract of employment if the reason for them is not connected with the transfer. However, if employees decides not to accept the changes but to treat themselves as constructively dismissed as a result, claims for constructive dismissal can be made. Whether the dismissal will be automatically unfair will depend on the nature and extent of the changes.

There is no fixed period beyond which changes can be made to an employee's contract without it being linked to the transfer. The causal link will be more difficult to establish the longer the period of time between the transfer and the resultant changes (unless the link can be made). It is a question of fact whether the causal link actually exists.

A recent case involving attempts by a transferee to harmonise the terms and conditions of those who transfer with the existing employee has provided further clarification of the law. This was *Taylor* v. *Connex South Eastern Ltd* (EAT 1243/99, 5 July 2000). Taylor was a chartered accountant who was employed by British Rail. In 1996 the organisation was privatised and transferred to Connex South East. Mr Taylor was offered a new contract but no agreement was reached on terms and he continued to be employed under his old contract. Another part of British Rail was then sold to Connex South Central. The two Connex companies were linked by management and they decided to rationalise all their terms and conditions under a process that was called 'synergisation'. Mr Taylor was presented, without warning, with a new contract, which contained a number of new clauses to his detriment. He refused to sign them and was dismissed. It was held that this was not a dismissal by reason of redundancy. It was also not for some other substantial reason as he was only dismissed for refusing to accept new terms. It was held in the EAT that even though the dismissal took place two years after the date of the transfer, there had been no intervening event to break the chain of causation. In this case that Mr Taylor's refusal to sign the new contract was a matter that was connected with the transfer. His dismissal was therefore on the grounds of his refusal to accept new terms and conditions, which was a reason connected with the transfer, which made it an automatically unfair dismissal under TUPE reg. 8(1).

6.15   DISMISSALS AND RE-ENGAGEMENT AFTER TRANSFER

The courts will look carefully at redundancy situations and the offer of re-engagement on different terms to see if it is being used to get around the ruling of *Berriman* v. *Delabole Slate*. Two cases illustrate the court's attitude to such dismissals. In *Servicepoint Ltd* v. *Clynes & Wigfalls* (EAT, 15 April 1989) the facts of this case were that the applicant worked at a West Yorkshire depot. This contract did not have a mobility clause. When the transferee purchased the business the West Yorkshire depot was closed and all employees were offered work at the Manchester depot but on less favourable terms and conditions. It was held that the transferee's objective was to effect the standardisation of contracts and not to effect changes in the workforce.

In *Crawford* v. *Swinton Insurance Brokers Ltd* [1990] IRLR 42 following a relevant transfer, the transferee decided to change substantially a secretary's function. This involved giving her sales responsibilities and getting her to work in an office when previously she had worked from home. For good measure the transferee also took away her company car. The tribunal held that Ms Crawford had been constructively dismissed and that the principal reason for the dismissal was the transfer. The reason was an organisational reason entailing changes in the workforce under reg. 8(2) and was therefore potentially fair. The tribunal found the dismissal to be fair but on appeal to the EAT it was held that there could be changes in the function of the workforce if some people were kept on but were performing entirely different jobs. The EAT allowed the appeal to the extent that the tribunal had not made a finding as to whether the ETO reason was the principal reason for the dismissal. The case was remitted to the tribunal on this point.

The case of *Wilson v. St Helens Borough Council* [1998] IRLR 706, HL considered the situation where employees were dismissed before the transfer and then re-employed by the transferee on new terms and conditions of employment. Here St Helens Borough Council agreed to take control of the controlled community home if the running of the home involved no expense to them. The transferor county council indicated that it would redeploy only staff who wanted to stay with them and the staff who moved to the borough council would be dismissed when the county council ceased to be in control. On transfer of the 102 staff who applied for posts 76 were offered posts in the new structure on the borough council's terms and conditions, which did not include an extraneous duties allowance which had formerly been paid. Over a year after the transfer took place, the applicants brought proceedings under the Wages Act 1986.

In the Lords it was held that the dismissals were effective in bringing the old contracts to an end. Contracts offered by the transferee and accepted were binding on the employees. Lord Slynn's judgment held as follows:

1. If there is an alteration at the time of or after the relevant transfer and the reason for the alteration is connected with the transfer, the employee can either accept the new terms or reject the new terms and treat the new terms as a constructive dismissal.

    As the employees waited one year before lodging an application to the tribunal, there had been a break in the chain of causation between the transfer, the contractual change and the objection to the change. If the employees had objected to the change immediately, the outcome would have been different. Lord Slynn commented that if a transferee could not safely agree terms to bring the new employees into line with existing employees' standard terms and conditions of employment, that would discourage employers from taking over new businesses. He was, therefore, keen not to undermine the benefits of beneficial takeovers to save jobs as against the need to protect employees' rights.

2. The transferee could avail itself of the ETO defence as the number of employees at the school had been considerably reduced.

3. The transfer of an undertaking did not constitute the reasons for the variation, it was a variation 'to the same extent as it could have been with regard to the Transferor'. If a variation in contractual terms is not due to the transfer, it can be validly made by either the transferor or the transferee before or after the transfer. If a contractual change is made that is not due to the transfer it will *not* be automatically unfair. It will be subject to the normal rules relating to unfair dismissal. One must, therefore, look at the facts of the case as well as the proximity of the change to the transfer to see if the change has a casual link to the transfer itself.

In *Meade & Baxendale* v. *British Fuels Ltd* [1998] IRLR 706 the Lords held that an employee's agreement to accept new terms and conditions was binding, as the dismissals were effective. Lord Slynn commented that neither the transferor nor the transferee could use the transfer as justification for dismissal. In English law there would be no order for specific performance, the claim would be for damages and perhaps an order for reinstatement or re-engagement. The Directive's aim was to 'approximate' the laws of member states and its purpose was to safeguard an employee's rights on transfer. Those rights depended upon national law. The Directive did not create in Community law a right to continue in employment. It sought only to ensure that the employee had rights and remedies against the purchaser of a business.

Where there was a transfer and the transferee took on an employee, the contract was automatically transferred. Where the transferee did not take on employees who were dismissed on transfer, the dismissal was not a nullity but it was only the contractual rights that remained enforceable against the transferee.

The case law on the subject does not imply that a transferee actually has to take on an employee who has been dismissed as a result of the transfer. If the transferee does take on such employees, however, it takes them on the same terms and condition that the employees enjoyed with the transferor. If the transferee does not take on an employee then it must meet all of the transferor's contractual and statutory obligations unless:

(a) the employee objects to being employed by the transferee; or
(b) the principal reason for the dismissal was an ETO and the employee is not to be treated as unfairly dismissed.

Where a transferor and transferee agree to dismiss with a view to introducing changes to terms and conditions of employment, they may fall foul of reg. 12, which makes any attempt to contract out of the TUPE regulations void. However, as the House of Lords has now confirmed, such dismissals are not a nullity.

In *Cornwall County Care Ltd* v. *Brightman* [1998] IRLR 228, EAT employees in a council care home were transferred to a company formed by the council. The transfer was a cost cutting exercise and the company dismissed all the staff and took them on at lower wages. The employees claimed unfair dismissal under reg. 8(1) and also claimed that they were still employed by the transferee company on their old terms and conditions. The ETO defence was not argued. The company's main defence was that the dismissals were not transfer related. It was held that the dismissals were unfair but that the employees were not entitled to a declaration. The dismissals were effective in bringing their old terms sand conditions of employment to an end. The employees could not continue to be employed on their old terms and conditions, and new terms and conditions were valid and binding.

In *Collino* v. *Telecom Italia SpA* [2000] IRLR 788 it was confirmed by the ECJ that the Directive does not preclude the transferee altering the terms of the employment relationship where national law allows an alteration in situations other than the transfer of an undertaking. This endorses the ruling which was formulated in *Daddy's Dance Hall* (*Foreningen af Arbejdsledere i Danmark* v. *Daddy's Dance Hall A/S* [1988] IRLR 315, ECJ (C-324/86)) that post-transfer changes in terms of conditions of employment, including those in relation to protection against dismissal and conditions of remuneration, are permissible to the extent that they could previously have been changed by the transferor under national law provided that the transfer of the undertaking itself does not constitute the reason for the change.

6.16 MUTUALLY AGREED VARIATIONS IN CONTRACTUAL TERMS

In *Credit Suisse First Boston (Europe) Ltd* v. *Padiachy* [1998] IRLR 504 after a takeover of part of Barclays Bank, Credit Suisse entered into agreements with certain key employees to secure their continued services over the following 12-month period. The new terms included a beneficial bonus payment and temporary modifications to post-termination restrictions in the employees' existing contracts. The new terms were better but in place of the 12-month non-solicitation covenant, the new provision had a three-month non-competition covenant applying in the event of an employee leaving during the initial period following the transfer. The employees agreed the new terms and received the one-off payments and they then went to work for a rival during the period of the non-competition covenant. It was held in the High Court that as the reason for the changes were for a reason connected with the transfer, the detrimental non-competition covenant was void, even though, on balance the employees were better off.

In *Credit Suisse First Boston* v. *Lister (Europe) Ltd* [1998] IRLR 700, CA it was confirmed that where no dismissals had taken place, any variation that took place by reason of the transfer, which was detrimental to the employee, could not be enforced. (For the status and enforceability of detrimental changes when a dismissal takes place, the *Wilson* case will apply (see 6.15).) This will be the situation even if the employee is placed in a better position after the transfer.

The facts of the case were that L worked for BZW as head of the European Equities Division. Credit Suisse (CS) entered into negotiations with BZW key employees with a view to identifying key employees and agreeing terms. Agreements were made with 209 employees by way of retention letters which contained an agreement to pay the employees a retention award which was either a straight cash payment or the granting of phantom shares. Legal advice was also offered to those who required it before signing the agreement.

L signed the retention letter which contained an offer of a retention award of £625,000 in phantom shares and £2,000 in consideration for agreeing new terms in November 1997. Clause 6 of the new terms stated that L would be subject to a restriction to prevent him working for a competitor for a period of three months and it contained a non-solicitation clause. In L's contract with BZW, the transferor, there was no restriction in respect of working for a competitor. In May 1998 the business transferred and the retention letter took effect. L resigned in June 1998 and found a job with a competitor. CS attempted to seek an interlocutory injunction to restrain L from accepting employment with a competitor in breach of the clause contained in the retention letter.

The High Court refused to grant the injunction on the grounds that clause 6 of the retention letter was unenforceable under TUPE reg. 5. CS then appealed to the Court of Appeal which held that:

1. The contract was unenforceable by virtue of reg. 5 as the variation had taken place by reason of the transfer (even though, on balance, the employee was better off).
2. Employees are not entitled to waive rights conferred upon them by the terms of their contract with the transferor, even if, on balance they were better off. The Court must not conduct a balancing act.
3. L was not entitled to waive his rights under his contract with the transferor to work for a competitor after his contract had terminated. As the transferor could not have prevented L from working for a competitor, neither could the transferee.

LJ Clarke said that:

> It may be noted that there is nothing in Regulation 5 which expressly provides that the employee and the Transferee are not free to vary by agreement the terms of employment as transferred, either from the date of the transfer or thereafter. However Regulation 12 is in these terms 'any provision of any agreement (whether a contract of employment or not) shall be void in so far as it purports to exclude or limit the operation of Regulation 5, 8 or 10 . . . or to preclude any person from preventing a complaint to an employment tribunal under Regulation 11 above'.

It was said in the present case that the transfer was the reason to change the contract. As rights under reg. 5 are a matter of public policy, it is not permissible to derogate from them in a manner unfavourable to the employee. Employees are not entitled to waive rights conferred upon them by the Directive and those rights cannot be restricted, even with consent.

The above cases show that consensual changes made to contracts for a reason connected with a transfer are unenforceable. This also means that the parties are left with their original contracts under reg. 5.

6.17 CHANGES IN NON-CONTRACTUAL TERMS

The Acquired Rights Directive does not require a transferee employer to follow a non-contractual employment practice after a transfer. Employees who were retained on contracts incorporating a collective agreement before a transfer could not compel the transferee to recognise the collective agreement after the transfer as it was not a legally binding document. The case on this matter was *Ralton and others* v. *Havering College of FHE* [2001] IRLR 738 EAT. The facts of the case were that the employees were employed on one-year fixed term contracts which were renewed annually. The contracts were subject to terms agreed by collective bargaining with the trade unions called the Silver Book. In 1993 the college, which had been run by Havering Borough Council, was transferred to Havering College, a statutory corporation established under the Further and Higher Education Act 1992. The contracts were renewed for one year subject to the Silver Book provisions. In 1994 the employees then accepted terms that were not subject to the Silver Book provisions. No employee objected at the time but in September 1994 all three objecting employees signed a petition objecting saying that the new terms were unlawful under Community law. They applied to the tribunal under the Employment Rights Act 1996, s.11 for a declaration that their terms were subject to the Silver Book. All the parties to the proceedings accepted that there had been a transfer of an undertaking and that the Directive applied as Havering College was taken to be an emanation of the state.

It was held by the EAT that:

1. Under national law employers would not be bound to offer a renewal of a contract subject to Silver Book terms. As the Silver Book terms were deemed to be a collective agreements they were not found to be binding upon the transferee after the transfer as they were not contractual terms.

2. It was also argued by the employees that art. 4(2) protects an employee 'if the contract of employment or the employment relationship is terminated because the transfer involves a substantial change in working conditions detrimental to the employee'. The employees used this article to support their argument that they were entitled to their pre-transfer terms as they could not agree to a detrimental variation. The EAT did not accept this point as art. 4(2) did not cover circumstances where there had been a variation in terms and conditions of a continuing contract. It only covered circumstances arising from constructive dismissal.

3. It was also argued by the employees that the variation only had to be 'connected' with the transfer, not 'solely' by reason of the transfer. The EAT found that the words 'connected with the transfer' were considered to be a reference relating to dismissals under reg. 8. It was confirmed by the EAT that the Directive only protects employees from changes to their contracts motivated 'solely' by the fact of the transfer. This ruling now gives a window

of opportunity to transferees who are trying to negotiate post-transfer changes to terms and conditions of employment.

6.18 COMPROMISE AGREEMENTS

Regulation 12 makes any agreement void in so far as it purports to limit the operation of reg. 8. However, employees can waive their rights to make a claim for unfair dismissal under the Employment Rights Act 1996, s.203, where employees have received independent legal advice from a qualified lawyer covered by a professional indemnity policy of insurance or via assistance through ACAS for the resolution of an industrial dispute. Would a compromise agreement under s.203 be a valid way of excluding an employee's right to lodge a claim in respect of a transfer-related dismissal or any other claim that arose on transfer?

Comparing the legislative status of the provisions involved, a regulation is inferior to an Act of Parliament, therefore TUPE reg. 12 would be interpreted in accordance with the superior status of the Employment Rights Act 1996. This leads to the view that a compromise agreement would be an effective way of settling an employee's prospective claims against a transferor or transferee. TUPE reg. 12 does not in any way water down the effectiveness of a compromise agreement. It must therefore be presumed that reg. 12 will only apply to any other form of agreement which is not drafted in accordance with the strict rules in s.203.

How, then, do the provisions of the Employment Rights Act 1996, s.203 conflict with the superior provisions of the Directive? Article 2(2) states that 'This Directive shall be without prejudice to National Law as regards the definition of contract of employment or employment relationship'. The provisions go on to specify when member states shall not exclude contracts of employment from the scope of the Directive. They include contracts such as fixed duration contracts, contracts for specified hours and part-time contracts. It is therefore clear that the enforceability of compromise agreements is not in conflict with the provisions of the Directive.

This interpretation of the enforceability of compromise agreements was confirmed in the case of *Milligan v. Securicor* [1995] IRLR 288, EAT where it was found that the TUPE regulations were not intended to give employees more extensive rights than employees unfairly dismissed for other reasons. In *Milligan*, the employee had insufficient continuous employment to lodge a claim for unfair dismissal and it was held that he could not lodge a claim for a transfer-related reason if he could not sustain a claim for unfair dismissal for any other reason. Taking this case into account, it seems likely that national law not only sets down minimum periods for statutory protection under the Employment Relations Act, but it also allows the parties effectively to reach a compromise agreement on those claims if certain provisions are followed. As long as these rules are followed, such agreements would be enforceable and in accordance with the spirit and letter of the superior provisions contained in the Directive.

There has been one case on the enforceability of compromise agreements where there is a transfer to which the TUPE regulations apply. This is *Thompson & Others* v. *Walon Car Delivery and BRS Automotive Limited* [1997] IRLR 343. The facts of the case were that BRS had a car distribution agreement with Saab. The Saab contract then went to Walon from the 30 January 1995. Walon claimed that the TUPE regulations did not apply and said that it would not employ BRS employees. BRS, therefore, negotiated with the employees for their contracts to come to an end on the 27 January 1995. BRS produced a compromise agreement but there was confusion on the issue of legal advice and the compromise agreements were not signed until the 1 February with the assistance of an ACAS officer. All the employees received a severance payment. The employees then brought a claim against Walon for unfair dismissal.

The EAT held that as the dismissals were effected because of the transfer, the transferors were liable for the unfair dismissal and that liability passed to the transferee under reg. 5. The settlement agreed by the transferor with the employees *after* the transfer could not benefit the transferees, who were not party to the agreement. At the time of signing the agreements on the 1 February, BRS was no longer the employer as under reg. 5 all rights and obligations of the employees had transferred across to the transferee. The transfer occurred on 30 January, days before the compromise agreement was signed. As the transferee was not party to the compromise agreement it could not argue that there was privity of contract to enable it them to take the benefit of the agreement to which it was not a party. The case was, therefore, referred to the tribunal for a hearing on its merits.

It was argued in the course of this decision whether the settlement agreements were void by reason of reg. 12. It was held that if a dismissal was deemed to be unfair under reg. 8(1), it would, therefore, be taken to be dealt with under the Employment Rights Act 1996,

Part X and, therefore, any compromise of a claim under the Act would be enforceable and binding under s.203. The EAT said that the parties should not be deprived of the help of dispute resolution by ACAS.

Take this decision into account it is seen that compromise agreements under s.203 will be binding, but in order for the transferee to take the benefit of them under reg. 5 they must be effective before the transfer. If there is any delay in signing the compromise agreement it may be signed after the date of legal transfer and if it is signed after this stage it should also be signed by the transferee in order to show that it is a party to the agreement and, therefore, had benefit of that agreement. An example of a typical tripartite compromise agreement appears at Appendix 7.

6.19 PUBLIC CONSULTATION DOCUMENT

It has now been confirmed in the DTI public consultation document on the TUPE regulations (see Appendix 4, paras. 23–5) that any changes to employees' contractual terms and conditions that are made for a valid ETO will be lawful and enforceable. This will be subject to the normal conditions that would apply irrespective of the transfer. It is expected that the Regulations will be redrafted to give effect to this clarification.

6.20 ADVICE ON TERMINATION

Advising the transferor

Where dismissals have taken place in connection with, or proximate to the transfer, the advice that must be given to a transferor can be summarised as follows:

1. If the transferor dismisses those employees in the part that is retained then it will retain liability for the dismissal.
2. If the transferor dismisses those employees from the part that is to be transferred and the dismissals are for a reason connected with the transfer then liability will pass to the transferee under reg. 5 All these dismissals must be covered by the terms of a compromise agreement in order to protect the transferor and the transferee, subject to the provisions contained in reg. 12. The compromise agreement should be signed before the transfer date

in order for the transferee to take the benefit of the agreement on transfer.

3. The transferor may face claims from dismissed employees for automatic unfair dismissal under the following circumstances:
   (a) if the employee has one year's service or more;
   (b) if the dismissal was for a reason related to the transfer.

   Under these circumstances the transferor may be able to avail itself of the defence of an ETO

4. If the transferor dismisses for a reason that is not connected with the transfer, the dismissal will be subject to the rules relating to unfair dismissal under the Employment Rights Act 1996, s.98(4) and the liability will remain with the transferor.

5. The transferor should resist all requests by the transferee to dismiss employees before the transfer, unless the transferor itself has a valid ETO defence in respect of a particular employee's dismissal. The transferor's only obligation to the employees before transfer is to inform and consult.

6. If any employee objects to transferring, the transferor should advise him or her as to the effect of objecting (see 5.14) and then the employee will be deemed to have resigned.

7. Where the transferor is asked to dismiss employees by the transferee, but for a reason connected with the transfer, the dismissal will be effective to terminate the contract but it will be deemed to be automatically unfair. The liability for the dismissal will pass to the transferee as if the employee had been dismissed by the transferee.

Advising the transferee

If the transferee wishes to dismiss for a reason relating to the transfer this will be automatically unfair under reg. 8. The dismissal will take effect to terminate the contract and the dismissal will not be a nullity. The transferee also has the defence of ETO if it can be shown that the requisite conditions apply. The transferee must be advised to leave a sufficient gap between the date of the transfer and any subsequent dismissals in order to make it less likely that the court may conclude that the dismissals were for a reason connected with the transfer. If the dismissals are not found to be connected with the transfer they will not be deemed to be automatically unfair. There is no magic time limit beyond which the transferee will be safe from claims for automatic unfair dismissal. As Connex found, two years was not enough to break the causal connection between the transfer and the reason for the dismissal.

If the dismissals of employees take place sufficiently remotely from the transfer, the transferee will still be expected to follow fair procedures under the Employment Rights Act 1996, s.98(4), and if an employee is to be made redundant, fair redundancy procedures, including the obligation to inform and consult employees, must be followed. It is also essential for the transferee to go through all necessary hearings and appeals before deciding to move to dismissal, otherwise the dismissal may still be held to be procedurally unfair. All dismissals should also be covered, if at all possible, by a compromise agreement in order to avoid the possibility of any tribunal applications.

Where the transferee wishes to harmonise employees' contractual terms and conditions of employment, which may include non-contractual procedural documents such as the staff handbook and attendance procedures, talks should have commenced with the transferring employees before the transfer and during the information and consultation stage. If terms need to be harmonised the less favourable terms should be improved upwards to align with the better terms and conditions, otherwise the employees who have their terms and conditions reduced would have valid claims under the Wages Act 1986 (as amended) and for breach of contract. Changes to payment terms and conditions do not constitute an ETO defence without the necessary change in size and job function of the workforce.

It is important that the following steps are taken by the transferee prior to harmonising the terms and conditions of employment in order to prevent claims for breach of contract or unfair dismissal arising:

1. There must be a valid ETO to support the change in contractual terms if the reason is connected with the transfer.
2. The correct contractual notice must be given to change the employees' contractual terms. The notice given may be contractual or statutory – whichever is the longer.
3. The new terms and conditions of employment must be placed before all the employees.
4. Employees should be encouraged to voice concerns and to sign the new terms and conditions within the notice period allowed.
5. If employees refuse the new terms and conditions it should be made clear that they will face dismissal. Dissenting employees would then have a claim for unfair dismissal but the transferee would have a defence of an ETO. The employees may face the

problem of being awarded a nil compensatory award for failure to mitigate (by not accepting the new terms). In addition, there will be no claim for wrongful dismissal as the correct contractual notice was given.

6. If the change in contractual terms is not connected with the transfer, ordinary principles of contract law and unfair dismissal apply. The TUPE regulations and the Directive will not apply.

In the light of the *Connex* case, the transferee must, however, exercise caution when imposing new terms and conditions as it may be likely that any attempt to harmonise terms and conditions for a reason connected with the transfer may render the subsequent dismissal automatically unfair and any change in the contractual terms void unless an ETO can be shown. There is no magic formula for deciding this issue and the best advice has to be to consult and seek agreement from the workforce and then cover any changes with a compromise agreement. The only way to avoid a conclusion that a change was imposed as a direct result of the transfer is to introduce variations that affect all of the workforce, including both the transferred and existing employees. The transferee may then have more evidence to show that the changes were for business grounds and not related to the transfer.

Advising the employee

Where an employee has been dismissed for a reason connected with the transfer, the employee needs to be advised of the provisions of reg. 8 as such a dismissal is automatically unfair if the employer does not have an ETO defence. The ETO defence will not make the dismissal fair, only not automatically unfair. The employer will still be expected to follow fair procedures and act in accordance with the contractual terms in order to terminate the contract effectively. The claim that would be lodged in order to protect the employee's position would be a claim for unfair dismissal against the dismissing employer. If the termination occurred before the transfer but for a reason connected with it then the claim would be against the transferee as reg. 5 and reg. 8 would be read together in order to transfer the employee rights across (as in the case of *Litster*).

If the dismissal were before the date of the transfer but for a reason not connected with it, or if there was doubt as to whether the dismissal were in connection with the transfer or if the dismissing employer had an ETO, the claim may merely subsist against the transferor alone. If there is doubt as to whether the dismissing employer had an effective ETO or if the dismissal were in connection with the transfer it may be prudent to lodge proceedings against both transferor and transferee to protect the employee's interests. The maximum compensation that could be claimed for automatically unfair dismissal would be the basic award together with the compensatory award (maximum £52,600).

The employee should also be advised to make any further claims against either the transferor or the transferee that may be subsisting at the date of dismissal and these will include those in respect of:

(a) the right to receive a written notification of changes in contractual terms under the Employment Rights Act 1996;
(b) breach of contract claims in respect of pay for notice period;
(c) Wages Act claims for moneys unlawfully deducted from pay;
(d) pay in respect of Working Time Regulation 1998 holidays;
(e) any discrimination claims that may be in existence at the effective date of termination.

Advising an employee at the date of dismissal or on the date of redundancy is relatively easy. Advising an employee in a transfer situation when the transferee is proposing changes in contractual terms is slightly more difficult as the cost of any claim that an employee has should be weighed against the value of continuing employment.

When, in the course of a transfer, the transferee is offering employment but on amended or 'harmonised' terms and conditions of employment, the employee has to be advised that:

1. If the 'harmonisation' was related to the transfer it would be void and unenforceable.
2. If the employee refused he or she could object to the change and might be entitled to treat him or herself as dismissed (constructive dismissal) either before the transfer and bring a claim against the transferor if the breach by the employer was a repudiatory breach under reg. 5, or after the transfer and bring a claim against the transferee.
3. The employer may have a defence to a redundancy, dismissal or constructive dismissal claim that it was an ETO.
4. If the defence succeeds, the employer only needs show that it acted as a reasonable employer in relying upon that reason, as the reason to dismiss. Reorganisation, redundancy and introducing new technology are likely to be three fair reasons to dismiss.

5. If the employee is successful in a claim for unfair dismissal it is under the usual duty to mitigate. The tribunal will take into account whether it was reasonable for the employee to refuse the harmonised terms or new terms and conditions. If the tribunal held that the dismissal was unfair but that the employee failed to act reasonably in refusing suitable alternative employment, the compensation may be reduced substantially (sometimes by 100 per cent).

6. The employee must therefore be made aware of the risks of litigation and the difficulty associated with bringing claims under the TUPE regulations. Although the employee's rights are protected, the compensation that may be awarded to an employee as a direct result of a breach of the regulations may be small. Although the TUPE regulations make a dismissal automatically unfair and thus place the burden of proof on the employer, they do not give the employee any additional employment based rights or protections. A dismissal will still be a dismissal. Jobs are not preserved, and only the value of contractual and statutory rights are protected. The only value of a claim is the compensation that can be awarded. Most employees would consider (or have to accept) that continued employment and job security was preferable to a constructive or actual dismissal with the prospect of six months or more of litigation, with the dangers, costs and uncertainties that this may hold.

CHAPTER 7

Pensions

7.1 PROVISIONS OF THE DIRECTIVE AND TUPE

Under art. 3(4)(a) of the Directive it is stated that:

> Unless Member States provide otherwise [the Directive] shall not apply in relation to employees' rights to old age, invalidity or survivors' benefits under supplementary company or inter company pension schemes outside the statutory social security schemes in the Member states.

Article 3(4)(b) states that:

> Even where they do not provide in accordance with paragraph (a) that [the Directive] apply in relation to such rights, Member States shall adopt the measures necessary to protect the interests of employees and of persons no longer employed in the transferor's business at the time of the transfer in respect of rights conferred on them immediate or prospective entitlement to old age benefits, including survivors' benefits under supplementary schemes referred to in subparagraph (a).

TUPE reg. 7(1) states:

> Regulation 5 and 6 . . . shall not apply
>
> (a) to so much of a contract of employment or collective agreement as relates to an occupational pension scheme within the meaning of the Social Security Pension Act 1975 or the Social Security Pensions (Northern Ireland) Order 1975 or
> (b) to any rights, powers duties or liabilities under or in connection with any such contract or subsisting by virtue of any such agreement and relating to such a scheme or otherwise arising in connection with that person's employment and relating to such a scheme.
> (c) For the purposes of paragraph (1) above any provisions of an occupational pension scheme which do not relate to benefits for old age invalidity or survivors shall not be treated as not being part of the scheme.

Regulation 7 therefore provides that reg. 5 shall not apply to that part of the contract of employment which relates to an occupational pension scheme. Occupational pension schemes therefore do not transfer and the transferee is free to choose whether to continue the scheme, begin a new one or offer no scheme at all, save for a stakeholder pension scheme.

7.2 PENSIONS AFTER THE TRANSFER

Two cases have made reference to art. 3(4)(b) of the Directive. Their pleadings have attempted to put forward the view that the provision places an obligation upon the transferee to provide a comparable pension benefit to that provided by the transferor. This has been held in both cases not to be the case. Article 3(4)(b) does not place an obligation on the employer in the private sector to provide a pension scheme.

In *Walden Engineering Co. Ltd* v. *Warrener* [1993] IRLR 420, EAT a contracted out pension scheme was deemed to be a supplementary scheme for the purposes of art. 3(4) of the Directive and therefore the scheme was excluded from its scope. The facts of the case were that Mr Warrener was employed in a company from 1980 and was part of a contracted out contributory pension scheme. In 1991 the business transferred to Walden Engineering (the transferee). The transferee arranged to cancel the contracting out certificate and contracted back into the state earnings related pension scheme (SERPS). The company pension was to be cancelled due to the excessive cost of maintaining it. Mr Warrener presented a claim to the employment tribunal for a declaration as to what the terms and conditions of employment were in relation to the pension scheme. The issue before the tribunal was whether the case of *Litster* argued that a purposive construction should be given to the Directive as to the second limb of the article, which expects member states to adopt protective measures in respect of employee rights which confer upon them 'immediate or prospective entitlement to old age benefits, including survivors benefits under supplementary schemes'.

Mr Warrener submitted that although reg. 7 did not give him a right to remain a member of the pension scheme, it did require that he was entitled to the same or equivalent pension benefit terms as those to which he had been entitled prior to the transfer. He also argued that a contracted out pension scheme was not a supplementary scheme under the article as it stood in substitution for the state scheme.

In the EAT it was held that:

1. Contracted out contributory pension schemes are supplementary pension schemes under the Directive. They therefore fall outside of the protection afforded by the Directive.
2. The second limb of the article does not advocate any liability on the transferor and the transferee in the private sector. It merely indicates that member states have a duty to protect the interests that crystallise on transfer.
3. An occupational pension scheme is excluded by reg. 7 from the automatic transfer provisions.

The second case that considered whether occupational pensions transfer to the transferee after a relevant transfer was *Adams* v. *Lancashire County Council* [1997] IRLR 436. The local authority operated a school catering service. The employees working in this service were entitled to join the pension scheme. The service was then contracted out to BET. The TUPE regulations applied to the transfer but BET could not afford to offer access to a pension scheme for any employee earning less than £15,000 per annum. The employees who could not afford to join the pension scheme commenced proceedings in the High Court. They claimed that they were entitled to equivalent pension rights after the transfer. The employees argued that the intention of the Directive was to protect the pay and conditions of workers when their employment was transferred to a new employer. As a pension was a form of 'deferred pay', the transferee's refusal to offer pension rights meant that the employees would be worse off in pay than they were before the transfer. Such unfairness was contrary to the general purpose of the Directive. The employees also made the point that the second limb of art. 3(4) provided that employees were entitled to the same level of pension benefits after the transfer.

In the Court of Appeal it was held that:

1. Following a transfer, the employees were not entitled to a comparable pension from the transferee as they had been entitled to from the transferor.
2. The first limb of the Directive provides that all pension rights are excluded from its operation.
3. The second limb of art. 3 of the Directive is addressed to member states and it is clear that it is dealing with accrued rights in respect of periods of pensionable service accruing prior to the transfer. It is not concerned with future rights after the transfer.

4. The second limb of art. 3 does not impose an obligation on the transferee to set up a pension scheme for the employees. The article does not require member states to adopt measures for the preservation of employees' rights to future benefits.

It is clear from the above case law that art. 3(4) and TUPE reg. 7 only preserve an employee's pension rights that crystallise on transfer. There is no obligation on a transferee to provide a pension for an employee who was in a pension scheme before the transfer.

7.3 OTHER BENEFITS ATTACHED TO THE PENSION SCHEME

Where the pension scheme contains other benefits that are not old age benefits or survivors benefits, these rights are capable of transferring. The TUPE regulations were amended by the Trade Union Reform and Employment Rights Act 1993. The Act inserted clause 7(2) to clarify the point. There has been two cases on this point, the first being *Frankling* v. *BPS Public Sector Ltd* [1999] IRLR 212, EAT. Employees worked in the Eastbourne Hospital NHS Trust on Whitley Council terms and conditions of employment. Under these terms and conditions of employment there was a condition for the making of enhanced redundancy payments and additional benefits under the NHS occupational pension scheme. It allowed employees who were over the age of 50 with more than five years' pension contributions to take their pension early. The pension scheme was in accordance with the Superannuation Act 1972, so the scheme had statutory status.

In 1996 the trust contracted out the payroll department to BPS and in 1997 the employees were made redundant. BPS paid the enhanced redundancy payment but not the additional benefits under the occupational pension scheme. The employees argued before the EAT that the payments were essentially compensation for the loss of a job and that early retirement provisions could reduce or extinguish the redundancy payments and they were therefore meant to be read together to provide a single redundancy provision. The employees argued that the provisions were not for 'old age, invalidity or survivors' but for redundancy purposes and therefore reg. 7 did not apply. BPS argued that the benefits under the pension scheme fell within reg. 7 and that because the pension was payable under a statutory scheme they were not benefits payable under a contract of employment. As the applicants had no contractual rights to those benefits when they worked for the NHS, they had no contractual right when they transferred to BPS.

It was held in the EAT that:

1. The transferee was not obliged to pay the enhanced early retirement benefits.
2. The provisions relating to early retirement were implemented by statutory regulation and not by contractual provision.
3. The pension was provided under a tripartite agreement where the employee, under statute, was entitled to receive payments from the scheme and the scheme was under a duty to make the payments. The transferor was under a duty to make payments under the scheme. There was no implied contractual term that the transferor was under an obligation to the employee to pay the benefits. There was no need to imply a term as the employee had a statutory right to the benefits.
4. As the transferor had no contractual liability to make the payment, no such obligation transferred.
5. The benefits under the scheme fell within the definition of an occupational pension scheme and would therefore be excluded.
6. The pension scheme did not cease to be a benefit for old age merely because the employees had not taken retirement at the normal retiring age. A benefit did not change its character or identity merely because it was enhanced or accelerated.
7. The applicants were therefore treated as retirees in order to give them benefits under the statutory pension scheme as the benefits were calculated by reference to age and years of service and were transmissible to survivors on death. They therefore fell within reg. 7 and were excluded from the transfer.

The same issues arose in the case of *Beckmann* v. *Dynamco Whicheloe Macfarlane Ltd* (C-164/00) (ECJ, June 2002). In this case Mrs Beckmann, who was a member of a national health service pension scheme had her contract transferred to a private company in 1995. She was then made redundant in 1997. Had she not transferred, she would have been entitled to certain benefits from the national health service scheme on redundancy together with enhancement. The transferee did not provide those benefits. The transferee argued that the TUPE regulations, which implemented the Acquired Rights Directive, did not transfer rights under an occupational pension scheme. Mrs Beckmann argued that the right she was claiming arose from the mode of her dismissal and, therefore, did not fall within the exemption of pension scheme rights. It was held by the ECJ that:

> Early retirement benefits and benefits intended to enhance the conditions of such retirement, paid in the event of dismissal to employees who have reached a certain age . . . are not old age . . . benefits within the meaning of pension exemption.

In the view of the ECJ it is only:

> benefits paid from time to time when an employee reaches the end of his or her working life as laid down by the general structure of the pension scheme in question and not benefits paid in circumstances such as those in the point in the main proceedings (dismissal for redundancy) that can be classed as old age benefits, even if they are calculated by reference to the rules for calculating normal pension schemes.

When one looks at the Government Consultation Document at Appendix 4 it is clear that the TUPE regulations will in future provide for such benefits to transfer across with a TUPE transfer.

The regulations do not however apply to transfer the right to continue active membership of an occupational pension scheme. It will also not transfer group life assurance benefits. An employee's accrued rights are protected by separate pension regulations.

It is apparent from the above case law that pension provisions in the event of a relevant transfer are treated differently depending on whether they concern public sector employees or private sector employees. The differences are outlined below.

7.4   PUBLIC SECTOR EMPLOYEES

It is government policy that former public sector employees who transfer to the private sector should continue to have provision made for them in respect of pension rights. The government's consultation paper (see Appendix 4, paras. 13–15) voices concern that unless a transferee provides similar or a comparable pension benefit to a transferring public sector employee, the government runs the real risk of a claim for constructive unfair dismissal. This concern arose out of the ruling in *University of Oxford* v. *Humphreys and the AEB* [2000] IRLR 183, CA (see p.96), where the failure of the transferee to provide a pension after the transfer allowed the employee to resign and claim constructive unfair dismissal against the transferor.

Central government gives guidance to government departments and local authorities stating clearly that a transferee from the public sector is generally required to offer transferred employees occupational pension provision 'broadly comparable' to that afforded by the transferor (see Chapter 3 on new guidance on public sector transfers and the public consultation document in Appendix 4). The Treasury has reaffirmed the position in a note entitled 'Staff transfers from central government: a fair deal for staff pensions'. The government actuarial department has set out an approach in order to test as to whether a pension provision is 'broadly comparable'. It is therefore clear that there is significantly greater protection for public sector employees than for private sector employees.

Private sector employees are clearly at a disadvantage as compared to public sector employees. The consultation document (see Appendix 4) has put forward a proposal to extend the protection of the TUPE regulations for occupational pension schemes for private sector employees. A number of proposals are put forward in para. 16 of the document, which include a one-off payment in compensation in exceptional circumstances where it was not reasonably practicable to provide a comparable pension scheme. Whatever approach is adopted by the government, it appears that there will be some protection for employees' pension rights in the event of a transfer in the future.

The commitment to reversing the decision in *Frankling* shows the direction that the government is following. The right to take early retirement on redundancy will shortly be a right that is transferred under reg. 5 and will no longer be excluded under reg. 7. There is also a commitment from the government to provide for the future benefits of an employee who enjoyed an occupational pension scheme with the transferor. All transfers may now have to contemplate the cost of transferring any potential pension liability of employees or to compensate for failing to provide a comparable benefit. Obviously, if the transferor does not provide a pension there will be no obligation on a transferee to provide anything after the transfer. The only obligation in such circumstances will be to provide a stakeholder pension, if the relevant provisions apply.

7.5 APPLICABILITY OF TUPE

Personal pension schemes

A personal pension is built around a direct contractual relationship between the individual and the pension scheme provider. There may also be a contractual agreement between the employer and the employee that the employer will contribute to the scheme. These schemes will form part of an employee's contractual rights that will transfer under the regulations.

Private health insurance schemes

Permanent health or prolonged disability schemes allow those who are long-term sick to receive an income and remain on the payroll. If the employer then transfers the business to the transferee the PHI scheme may not follow the employee. If an employee is off sick at the time of the transfer and the medical condition arose out of the actionable negligence of the transferor, that liability will transfer to the transferee, as was held in the cases of *Bernadone* v. *Pall Mall Services Group and Others* and *Martin* v. *Lancashire County Council* [2000] IRLR 487, CA, where it was held that the tortious liability of the transferor passed to the transferee and with it the benefit of any insurance policy. The transferor has a contingent or vested right to recover from an insurance policy taken out in respect of liability to employees in the workplace and these rights should transfer to the transferee.

If the transferor offers such a policy and the transferee decides upon financial or other grounds that a comparable provision will not be made available to employees after the transfer, it is clear that reg. 5 will not transfer the employees' rights across, as the current reg. 7 will apply to any provision made for invalidity benefit. However, what is not clear is the extent to which an employee could argue constructive unfair dismissal against the transferor and refuse to transfer. This would be particularly relevant for an employee who had received benefits under a scheme and would be likely to need to make an additional or continuing claim and who might excluded from a new scheme that excluded pre-existing medical conditions. There is no easy way around this problem and the transferor and the transferee will have to consult with any employees who have, or are likely to have, long-term medical conditions that might result in a claim on a policy. They must decide whether, after medical opinion, it would be better for the employee to transfer to the transferee or to perhaps consider taking early retirement on the grounds of ill health (or perhaps staying in the employment of the transferor, if that were an option). Any decision taken must be after taking full medical advice and after seeking the agreement of the employee. Any decision not to transfer an employee on the grounds of a disability would be discrimination contrary to the Disability Discrimination Act 1995 and obviously any dismissal as a result of the transfer would also be automatically unfair. Under reg. 8 any decision taken must be made with full consideration of the insurance position and the effects that this will have on the employee's future rights. Unfortunately, the

Disability Discrimination Act does not apply to insurance policies, therefore an employer may be found to have been discriminating on the benefits that are afforded to an employee but an insurance company bears no risk of a claim if it excludes a transferring employee on the grounds of a pre-existing medical condition.

Stakeholder pensions

From October 2001 all employers who employ more than five employees will be required to make stakeholder pensions available for their employees. These will not be occupational pension schemes and will therefore transfer across under the TUPE regulations.

Advice to the transferor

1. If the transferor does not provide an occupational pension scheme, there is no obligation on the transferee to provide one.
2. If the transferor does provide an occupational pension scheme to its employees, the following should be taken into consideration:

    (a) if the transferee does not provide a pension, advice must be given to the transferor as to the likelihood of a claim for constructive unfair dismissal being made by the employee (pursuant to reg. 5(5));
    (b) if the scheme provides for early retirement on the grounds of redundancy, or some other early retirement provisions, this may transfer to the transferee when the TUPE regulations have been amended in accordance with the consultation document (Appendix 4). The provisions of the scheme should therefore be provided to the transferee for them to take a view;
    (c) if the transferee also provides an occupational pension scheme accurate advice should be given on the comparative values of each scheme. If errors are made on comparative values, employees may have a claim under negligent misstatement, as in the case of Howard Hagen v. ICI Chemicals and Kvaemer Engineering (19 October 2001). It may be prudent for both the transferor and the transferee to obtain independent actuarial advice on a comparison for pension scheme values.
3. If any employee is off sick and is receiving benefit via a PHI scheme, the transferor must consult with the insurance provider

regarding the transfer, to secure the rights of those already receiving benefits. If an employee has received benefits from a PHI scheme and is likely to require further time off for a long-term medical condition, the transferor should:

(a)   consult with the employee,
(b)   consult with the insurance company,
(c)   consult with the transferee,

as to the best way forward to protect the employee's future interests. Any decision taken without taking into account the representations of the employee could result in a claim for con-structive unfair dismissal (or disability discrimination against the transferee if a decision is taken not to transfer the employee).

4.   All the information regarding pensions, PHI and other employee benefits must be provided by the transferor to the transferee in order for the transferee to decide what comparable benefits can be provided. If comparable benefits cannot be provided, this will amount to a 'measure' to be taken by the transferee in connec-tion with the transfer and will oblige the transferee and trans-feror to consult with the employees. (Although the duty rests upon the transferor before the transfer, it is always more effec-tive if joint negotiations can take place with all parties being present.)

Advice to the transferee

1.   There is no obligation presently upon the transferee to provide a comparable occupational pension scheme. If a pension scheme is provided, representations should not be made as to the comparative values of the transferee's scheme as these representations could later be relied upon by the employees. If comparisons are made, they should be provided by independent experts (who have the benefit of insurance).

2.   The transferee may be obliged to comply with an obligation to pay enhanced severance under an occupational pension scheme. The transferee should therefore obtain full details of any sever-ance terms in a pension scheme relating to early retirement (and also to secure an indemnity in respect of this contingent liability from the transferor).

3.   The transferee must obtain details of any PHI scheme or other benefit scheme dealing with disability. The transferee must establish the details of all the following categories of employee:

(a) those off sick due to the actionable negligence of the transferor, and obtain details of any insurance claim (or prospective claim);
(b) those off as long-term sick with a disability and receiving benefits (and details of any claim against an insurance policy);
(c) those who have been off on long-term sick leave with a disability but have since returned to work but are likely to require further time off in the future (together with details of the insurance policy, claim number and any medical details).

Once all of the above has been established, a view can be taken of the liabilities that will transfer and how best to deal with each category of employee.

Employees who are off sick and in receipt of benefits from an insurance provider under a company scheme can easily be overlooked by a transferor. It is therefore essential to establish who is 'on the books' at the date of the transfer in order to give contractual and statutory recognition to those who are employees.

Advice to employees

1. In order to advise employees, it must first be established what types of benefits are available to the employee in the transferor's establishment. As a general view, occupational pension schemes will not transfer, but benefits relating to severance may do so. Details of all schemes must be obtained before advice can be given.
2. Stakeholder and personal pensions will transfer.
3. If an employee deems the provisions of a pension to be critical to their terms and conditions of employment, to such an extent that the new terms or the identity of the transferee is significant and to the employee's detriment, the employee may have a right to claim under reg. 5(5) and treat him or herself as being constructively unfairly dismissed and claim against the transferor. If employees submit such a claim they could seek a remedy against the transferor in order to increase their potential contributions to the scheme. This would obviously depend upon the transferor being in existence after the transfer.
4. If misrepresentations are made before a transfer as to the comparative values of the transferor and transferee pension scheme, the employee may have a claim against both the transferor and transferee for negligent misstatement.

5. Where employees have the benefit of a PHI scheme provided by the transferor, similar benefits should be provided by the transferee. Failure to provide any contractual benefits may entitle an employee to claim automatically unfair dismissal against the transferee in respect of any detrimental changes in contractual benefits. The employer would be entitled to run a defence of an ETO in respect of changes in contractual terms.

The difficulty in advising an employee of the existence of such a right is the problem of then advising of the value of the claim as against the cost of proceeding with the claim and the risks that are involved. If employees treat themselves as dismissed, they will then be unemployed, and the cost involved in losing a job would be far in excess of the value of the benefit withdrawn. This as a stand-alone claim is rarely viable unless pension benefits are also included. This is why most claims relating to PHI and pension entitlement on transfer are supported by trade unions as they have the necessary resources to fund such claims on behalf of their members. Advice to employees as to their entitlement to retain such benefits should be pursued at the consultation stage in the hope of reaching settlement. Although legal remedies are available to employees to protect their terms and conditions of employment in regs. 5 and 8, the true cost of asserting those rights and the value of full-time employment should be looked at as part of the equation.

Council Directive 2001/23/EC (12 March 2001)

ON THE APPROXIMATION OF THE LAWS OF THE MEMBER STATES RELATING TO THE SAFEGUARDING OF EMPLOYEES' RIGHTS IN THE EVENT OF TRANSFERS OF UNDERTAKINGS, BUSINESSES OR PARTS OF UNDERTAKINGS OR BUSINESSES

The Council of the European Union,

Having regard to the Treaty establishing the European Community, and in particular Article 94 thereof,

Having regard to the proposal from the Commission,

Having regard to the opinion of the European Parliament,

Having regard to the opinion of the Economic and Social Committee,

Whereas:

(1) Council Directive 77/187/EEC of 14 February 1977 on the approximation of the laws of the Member States relating to the safeguarding of employees' rights in the event of transfers of undertakings, businesses or parts of undertakings or businesses has been substantially amended. In the interests of clarity and rationality, it should therefore be codified.

(2) Economic trends are bringing in their wake, at both national and Community level, changes in the structure of undertakings, through transfers of undertakings, businesses or parts of undertakings or businesses to other employers as a result of legal transfers or mergers.

(3) It is necessary to provide for the protection of employees in the event of a change of employer, in particular, to ensure that their rights are safeguarded.

(4) Differences still remain in the Member States as regards the extent of the protection of employees in this respect and these differences should be reduced.

(5) The Community Charter of the Fundamental Social Rights of Workers adopted on 9 December 1989 ('Social Charter') states, in points 7, 17 and 18 in particular that: 'The completion of the internal market must lead to an improvement in the living and working

conditions of workers in the European Community. The improvement must cover, where necessary, the development of certain aspects of employment regulations such as procedures for collective redundancies and those regarding bankruptcies. Information, consultation and participation for workers must be developed along appropriate lines, taking account of the practice in force in the various Member States. Such information, consultation and participation must be implemented in due time, particularly in connection with restructuring operations in undertakings or in cases of mergers having an impact on the employment of workers'.

(6) In 1977 the Council adopted Directive 77/187/EEC to promote the harmonisation of the relevant national laws ensuring the safeguarding of the rights of employees and requiring transferors and transferees to inform and consult employees' representatives in good time.

(7) That Directive was subsequently amended in the light of the impact of the internal market, the legislative tendencies of the Member States with regard to the rescue of undertakings in economic difficulties, the case-law of the Court of Justice of the European Communities, Council Directive 75/129/EEC of 17 February 1975 on the approximation of the laws of the Member States relating to collective redundancies and the legislation already in force in most Member States.

(8) Considerations of legal security and transparency required that the legal concept of transfer be clarified in the light of the case-law of the Court of Justice. Such clarification has not altered the scope of Directive 77/187/EEC as interpreted by the Court of Justice.

(9) The Social Charter recognises the importance of the fight against all forms of discrimination, especially based on sex, colour, race, opinion and creed.

(10) This Directive should be without prejudice to the time limits set out in Annex I [not included] Part B [not included] within which the Member States are to comply with Directive 77/187/EEC, and the act amending it,

Has Adopted this Directive:

Chapter I. Scope and definitions

Article 1

1. (a) This Directive shall apply to any transfer of an undertaking, business, or part of an undertaking or business to another employer as a result of a legal transfer or merger.

   (b) Subject to subparagraph (a) and the following provisions of this Article, there is a transfer within the meaning of this Directive where there is a transfer of an economic entity which retains its identity, meaning an organised grouping of resources which has the objective of pursuing an economic activity, whether or not that activity is central or ancillary.

(c) This Directive shall apply to public and private undertakings engaged in economic activities whether or not they are operating for gain. An administrative reorganisation of public administrative authorities, or the transfer of administrative functions between public administrative authorities, is not a transfer within the meaning of this Directive.

2. This Directive shall apply where and in so far as the undertaking, business or part of the undertaking or business to be transferred is situated within the territorial scope of the Treaty.

3. This Directive shall not apply to seagoing vessels.

Article 2

1. For the purpose of this Directive:

(a) 'transferor' shall mean any natural or legal person who, by reason of a transfer within the meaning of Article 1(1), ceases to be the employer in respect of the undertaking, business or part of the undertaking or business;

(b) 'transferee' shall mean any natural or legal person who, by reason of a transfer within the meaning of Article 1(1), becomes the employer in respect of the undertaking, business or part of the undertaking or business;

(c) 'representatives of employees' and related expressions shall mean the representatives of the employees provided for by the laws or practices of the Member States;

(d) 'employee' shall mean any person who, in the Member State concerned, is protected as an employee under national employment law.

2. This Directive shall be without prejudice to national law as regards the definition of contract of employment or employment relationship

However, Member States shall not exclude from the scope of this Directive contracts of employment or employment relationships solely because:

(a) of the number of working hours performed or to be performed,

(b) they are employment relationships governed by a fixed-duration contract of employment within the meaning of Article 1(1) of Council Directive 91/383/EEC of 25 June 1991 supplementing the measures to encourage improvements in the safety and health at work of workers with a fixed-duration employment relationship or a temporary employment relationship, or

(c) they are temporary employment relationships within the meaning of Article 1(2) of Directive 91/383/EEC, and the undertaking, business or part of the undertaking or business transferred is, or is part of, the temporary employment business which is the employer.

Chapter II. Safeguarding of employees' rights

Article 3

1. The transferor's rights and obligations arising from a contract of employment or from an employment relationship existing on the date of a transfer shall, by reason of such transfer, be transferred to the transferee.

Member States may provide that, after the date of transfer, the transferor and the transferee shall be jointly and severally liable in respect of obligations which arose before the date of transfer from a contract of employment or an employment relationship existing on the date of the transfer.

2. Member States may adopt appropriate measures to ensure that the transferor notifies the transferee of all the rights and obligations which will be transferred to the transferee under this Article, so far as those rights and obligations are or ought to have been known to the transferor at the time of the transfer. A failure by the transferor to notify the transferee of any such right or obligation shall not affect the transfer of that right or obligation and the rights of any employees against the transferee and/or transferor in respect of that right or obligation.

3. Following the transfer, the transferee shall continue to observe the terms and conditions agreed in any collective agreement on the same terms applicable to the transferor under that agreement, until the date of termination or expiry of the collective agreement or the entry into force or application of another collective agreement.

Member States may limit the period for observing such terms and conditions with the proviso that it shall not be less than one year.

4. (a) Unless Member States provide otherwise, paragraphs 1 and 3 shall not apply in relation to employees' rights to old-age, invalidity or survivors' benefits under supplementary company or intercompany pension schemes outside the statutory social security schemes in Member States.

   (b) Even where they do not provide in accordance with subparagraph (a) that paragraphs 1 and 3 apply in relation to such rights, Member States shall adopt the measures necessary to protect the interests of employees and of persons no longer employed in the transferor's business at the time of the transfer in respect of rights conferring on them immediate or prospective entitlement to old age benefits, including survivors' benefits, under supplementary schemes referred to in subparagraph (a).

Article 4

1. The transfer of the undertaking, business or part of the undertaking or business shall not in itself constitute grounds for dismissal by the transferor or the transferee. This provision shall not stand in the way of dismissals that may take place for economic, technical or organisational reasons entailing changes in the workforce.

Member States may provide that the first subparagraph shall not apply to certain specific categories of employees who are not covered by the laws or practice of the Member States in respect of protection against dismissal.

2. If the contract of employment or the employment relationship is terminated because the transfer involves a substantial change in working conditions to the detriment of the employee, the employer shall be regarded as having been responsible for termination of the contract of employment or of the employment relationship.

Article 5

1. Unless Member States provide otherwise, Articles 3 and 4 shall not apply to any transfer of an undertaking, business or part of an undertaking or business where the transferor is the subject of bankruptcy proceedings or any analogous insolvency proceedings which have been instituted with a view to the liquidation of the assets of the transferor and are under the supervision of a competent public authority (which may be an insolvency practitioner authorised by a competent public authority).

2. Where Articles 3 and 4 apply to a transfer during insolvency proceedings which have been opened in relation to a transferor (whether or not those proceedings have been instituted with a view to the liquidation of the assets of the transferor) and provided that such proceedings are under the supervision of a competent public authority (which may be an insolvency practitioner determined by national law) a Member State may provide that:

(a) notwithstanding Article 3(1), the transferor's debts arising from any contracts of employment or employment relationships and payable before the transfer or before the opening of the insolvency proceedings shall not be transferred to the transferee, provided that such proceedings give rise, under the law of that Member State, to protection at least equivalent to that provided for in situations covered by Council Directive 80/987/EEC of 20 October 1980 on the approximation of the laws of the Member States relating to the protection of employees in the event of the insolvency of their employer, and, or alternatively, that,

(b) the transferee, transferor or person or persons exercising the transferor's functions, on the one hand, and the representatives of the employees on the other hand may agree alterations, in so far as current law or practice permits, to the employees' terms and conditions of

151

employment designed to safeguard employment opportunities by ensuring the survival of the undertaking, business or part of the undertaking or business.

3. A Member State may apply paragraph 20(b) to any transfers where the transferor is in a situation of serious economic crisis, as defined by national law, provided that the situation is declared by a competent public authority and open to judicial supervision, on condition that such provisions already existed in national law on 17 July 1998.

The Commission shall present a report on the effects of this provision before 17 July 2003 and shall submit any appropriate proposals to the Council.

4. Member States shall take appropriate measures with a view to preventing misuse of insolvency proceedings in such a way as to deprive employees of the rights provided for in this Directive.

Article 6

1. If the undertaking, business or part of an undertaking or business preserves its autonomy, the status and function of the representatives or of the representation of the employees affected by the transfer shall be preserved on the same terms and subject to the same conditions as existed before the date of the transfer by virtue of law, regulation, administrative provision or agreement, provided that the conditions necessary for the constitution of the employee's representation are fulfilled.

The first subparagraph shall not supply if, under the laws, regulations, administrative provisions or practice in the Member States, or by agreement with the representatives of the employees, the conditions necessary for the reappointment of the representatives of the employees or for the reconstitution of the representation of the employees are fulfilled.

Where the transferor is the subject of bankruptcy proceedings or any analogous insolvency proceedings which have been instituted with a view to the liquidation of the assets of the transferor and are under the supervision of a competent public authority (which may be an insolvency practitioner authorised by a competent public authority), Member States may take the necessary measures to ensure that the transferred employees are properly represented until the new election or designation of representatives of the employees.

If the undertaking, business or part of an undertaking or business does not preserve its autonomy, the Member States shall take the necessary measures to ensure that the employees transferred who were represented before the transfer continue to be properly represented during the period necessary for the reconstitution or reappointment of the representation of employees in accordance with national law or practice.

2. If the term of office of the representatives of the employees affected by the transfer expires as a result of the transfer, the representatives shall

continue to enjoy the protection provided by the laws, regulations, administrative provisions or practice of the Member States.

Chapter III. Information and consultation

Article 7

1. The transferor and transferee shall be required to inform the representatives of their respective employees affected by the transfer of the following:

– the date or proposed date of the transfer,
– the reasons for the transfer,
– the legal, economic and social implications of the transfer for the employees,
– any measures envisaged in relation to the employees.

The transferor must give such information to the representatives of his employees in good time, before the transfer is carried out.

The transferee must give such information to the representatives of his employees in good time, and in any event before his employees are directly affected by the transfer as regards their conditions of work and employment.

2. Where the transferor or the transferee envisages measures in relation to his employees, he shall consult the representatives of this employees in good time on such measures with a view to reaching an agreement.

3. Member States whose laws, regulations or administrative provisions provide that representatives of the employees may have recourse to an arbitration board to obtain a decision on the measures to be taken in relation to employees may limit the obligations laid down in paragraphs 1 and 2 to cases where the transfer carried out gives rise to a change in the business likely to entail serious disadvantages for a considerable number of the employees.

The information and consultations shall cover at least the measures envisaged in relation to the employees.

The information must be provided and consultations take place in good time before the change in the business as referred to in the first subparagraph is effected.

4. The obligations laid down in this Article shall apply irrespective of whether the decision resulting in the transfer is taken by the employer or an undertaking controlling the employer.

In considering alleged breaches of the information and consultation requirements laid down by this Directive, the argument that such a breach occurred because the information was not provided by an undertaking controlling the employer shall not be accepted as an excuse.

5. Member States may limit the obligations laid down in paragraphs 1, 2 and 3 to undertakings or businesses which, in terms of the number of employees, meet the conditions for the election or nomination of a collegiate body representing the employees.

6. Member States shall provide that, where there are no representatives of the employees in an undertaking or business through no fault of their own, the employees concerned must be informed in advance of:

- the date or proposed date of the transfer,
- the reason for the transfer,
- the legal, economic and social implications of the transfer for the employees,
- any measures envisaged in relation to the employees.

Chapter IV. Final provisions

Article 8

This Directive shall not affect the right of Member States to apply or introduce laws, regulations or administrative provisions which are more favourable to employees or to promote or permit collective agreements or agreements between social partners more favourable to employees.

Article 9

Member States shall introduce into their national legal systems such measures as are necessary to enable all employees and representatives of employees who consider themselves wronged by failure to comply with the obligations arising from this Directive to pursue their claims by judicial process after possible recourse to other competent authorities.

Article 10

The Commission shall submit to the Council an analysis of the effect of the provisions of this Directive before 17 July 2006. It shall propose any amendment which may seem necessary.

Article 11

Member States shall communicate to the Commission the texts of the laws, regulations and administrative provisions which they adopt in the field covered by this Directive.

Article 12

Directive 77/187/EEC, as amended by the Directive referred to in Annex I [not included] Part A, is repealed, without prejudice to the obligations of the Member States concerning the time limits for implementation set out in Annex I, Part B.

References to the repealed Directive shall be construed as references to this Directive and shall be read in accordance with the correlation table in Annex II [not included].

Article 13

This Directive shall enter into force on the 20th day following its publication in the *Official Journal of the European Communities.*

Article 14

This Directive is addressed to the Member States.
Done at Brussels, 12 March 2001.

For the Council
The President
B. Ringholm

APPENDIX 2

Council Directive 2002/14/EC

ESTABLISHING A GENERAL FRAMEWORK FOR INFORMATION AND CONSULTING EMPLOYEES IN THE EUROPEAN COMMUNITY

The European Parliament and the Council of the European Union,

Having regard to the Treaty establishing the European Community, and in particular Article 137(2) thereof,

Having regard to the proposal from the Commission,

Having regard to the opinion of the Economic and Social Committee,

Having regard to the opinion of the Committee of the Regions,

Acting in accordance with the procedure referred to in Article 251, and in the light of the joint text approved by the Conciliation Committee on 23 January 2002,

Whereas:

(1) Pursuant to Article 136 of the Treaty, a particular objective of the Community and the Member States is to promote social dialogue between management and labour.

(2) Point 17 of the Community Charter of Fundamental Social Rights of Workers provides, *inter alia*, that information, consultation and participation for workers must be developed along appropriate lines, taking account of the practices in force in different Member States.

(3) The Commission consulted management and labour at Community level on the possible direction of Community action on the information and consultation of employees in undertakings within the Community.

(4) Following this consultation, the Commission considered that Community acton was advisable and again consulted management and labour on the contents of the planned proposal; management and labour have presented their opinions to the Commission.

(5) Having completed this second stage of consultation, management and labour have not informed the Commission of their wish to initiate the process potentially leading to the conclusion of an agreement.

(6) The existence of legal frameworks at national and Community level intended to ensure that employees are involved in the affairs of the undertaking employing them and in decisions affecting employees from being taken and made public without adequate procedures having been implemented beforehand to inform and consult them.

(7) There is a need to strengthen dialogue and promote mutual trust within undertakings in order to improve risk anticipation, make work organisation more flexible and facilitate employee access to training within the undertaking while maintaining security, make employees aware of adaptation needs, increase employees' availability to undertake measures and activities to increase their employability, promote employee involvement in the operation and future of the undertaking and increase its competitiveness.

(8) There is a need, in particular, to promote and enhance information and consultation on the situation and likely development of employment within the undertaking and, where the employer's evaluation suggests that employment within the undertaking may be under threat, the possible anticipatory measures envisaged, in particular in terms of employee training and skill development, with a view to offsetting the negative developments or their consequences and increasing the employability and adaptability of the employees likely to be affected.

(9) Timely information and consultation is a prerequisite for the success of the restructuring and adaptation of undertakings to the new conditions created by globalisation of the economy, particularly through the development of new forms of organisation of work.

(10) The Community has drawn up and implemented an employment strategy based on the concepts of 'anticipation', 'prevention' and 'employability', which are to be incorporated as key elements into all public policies likely to benefit employment, including the policies of individual undertakings, by strengthening the social dialogue with a view to promoting change compatible with preserving the priority objective of employment.

(11) Further development of the internal market must be properly balanced, maintaining the essential values on which our societies are based and ensuring that all citizens benefit from economic development.

(12) Entry into the third stage of economic and monetary union has extended and accelerated the competitive pressures at European level. This means that more supportive measures are needed at national level.

(13) The existing legal frameworks for employee information and consultation at Community and national level tend to adopt an excessively a posteriori approach to the process of change, neglect the economic aspects of decisions taken and do not contribute either to genuine anticipation of employment developments within the undertaking or to risk prevention.

(14) All of these political, economic, social and legal developments call for changes to the existing legal framework providing for the legal and practical instruments enabling the right to be informed and consulted to be exercised.

(15) This Directive is without prejudice to national systems regarding the exercise of this right in practice where those entitled to exercise it are required to indicate their wishes collectively.

(16) This Directive is without prejudice to those systems which provide for the direct involvement of employees, as long as they are always free to exercise the right to be informed and consulted through their representatives.

(17) Since the objectives of the proposed action, as outlined above, cannot be adequately achieved by the Member States, in that the object is to establish a framework for employee information and consultation appropriate for the new European context described above, and can therefore, in view of the scale and impact of the proposed action, be better achieved at Community level, the Community may adopt measures in accordance with the principle of subsidiary as set out in Article 5 of the Treaty. In accordance with the principle of proportionality, as set out in that Article, this Directive does not go beyond what is necessary in order to achieve these objectives.

(18) The purpose of this general framework is to establish minimum requirements applicable throughout the Community while not preventing Member States from laying down provisions more favourable to employees.

(19) The purpose of this general framework is also to avoid any administrative, financial or legal constraints which would hinder the creation and development of small and medium-sized undertakings. To this end, the scope of this Directive should be restricted, according to the choice made by Member States, to undertakings with at least 50 employees or establishments employing at least 20 employees.

(20) This takes into account and is without prejudice to other national measures and practices aimed at fostering social dialogue within companies not covered by this Directive and within public administrations.

(21) However, on a transitional basis, Member States in which there is no established statutory system of information and consultation of employees or employee representation should have the possibility of further restricting the scope of the Directive as regards the numbers of employees.

(22) A Community framework for informing and consulting employees should keep to a minimum the burden on undertakings or establishments while ensuring the effective exercise of the rights granted.

(23) The objective of this Directive is to be achieved through the establishment of a general framework comprising the principles, definitions and arrangements for information and consultation, which it will be for the Member States to comply with and adapt to their own national situation, ensuring, where appropriate, that management and labour have a leading role by allowing them to define freely, by agreement, the arrangements for informing and consulting employees which they consider to be best suited to their needs and wishes.

(24) Care should be taken to avoid affecting some specific rules in the field of employee information and consultation existing in some national laws, addressed to undertakings or establishments which pursue political, professional, organisational, religious, charitable, educational, scientific or artistic aims, as well as aims involving information and expression of opinions.

(25) Undertakings and establishments should be protected against disclosure of certain particularly sensitive information.

(26) The employer should be allowed not to inform and consult where this would seriously damage the undertaking or the establishment or where he has to comply immediately with an order issued to him by a regulatory or supervisory body.

(27) Information and consultation imply both rights and obligations for management and labour at undertaking or establishment level.

(28) Administrative or judicial procedures, as well as sanctions that are effective, dissuasive and proportionate in relation to the seriousness of the offence, should be applicable in cases of infringement of the obligations based on this Directive.

(29) This Directive should not affect the provisions, where these are more specific, of Council Directive 98/59/EC of 20 July 1998 on the approximation of the laws of the Member States relating to collective redundancies and of Council Directive 2001/23/EC of 12 March 2001 on the approximation of the laws of the Member States relating to the safeguarding of employees' rights in the event of transfers of undertakings, businesses or parts of undertakings or businesses.

(30) Other rights of information and consultation, including those arising from Council Directive 94/45/EEC of 22 September 1994 on the establishment of a European Works Council or a procedure in Community-scale undertakings and Community-scale groups of undertakings for the purposes of informing and consulting employees, should not be affected by this Directive.

(31) Implementation of this Directive should not be sufficient grounds for a reduction in the general level of protection of workers in the areas to which it applies,

Have adopted this directive:

Article 1. Object and principles

1. The purpose of this Directive is to establish a general framework setting out minimum requirements for the right to information and consultation of employees in undertakings or establishments within the Community.

2. The practical arrangements for information and consultation shall be defined and implemented in accordance with national law and industrial relations practices in individual Member States in such a way as to ensure their effectiveness.

3. When defining or implementing practical arrangements for information and consultation, the employer and the employees' representatives shall work in a spirit of cooperation and with due regard for their reciprocal rights and obligations, taking into account the interests both of the undertaking or establishment and of the employees.

Article 2. Definitions

For the purposes of this Directive:

(a) 'undertaking' means a public or private undertaking carrying out an economic activity, whether or not operating for gain, which is located within the territory of the Member States;

(b) 'establishment' means a unit of business defined in accordance with national law and practice, and located within the territory of a Member State, where an economic activity is carried out on an ongoing basis with human and material resources;

(c) 'employer' means the natural or legal person party to employment contracts or employment relationships with employees, in accordance with national law and practice;

(d) 'employee' means any person who, in the Member State concerned, is protected as an employee under national employment law and in accordance with national practice;

(e) 'employees' representatives' means the employees' representatives provided for by national laws and/or practices;

(f) 'information' means transmission by the employer to the employees' representatives of data in order to enable them to acquaint themselves with the subject matter and to examine it;

(g) 'consultation' means the exchange of views and establishment of dialogue between the employees' representatives and the employer.

Article 3. Scope

1. This Directive shall apply, according to the choice made by Member States, to:

(a) undertakings employing at least 50 employees in any one Member State, or

(b) establishments employing at least 20 employees in any one Member State.

Member States shall determine the method for calculating the thresholds of employees employed.

2. In conformity with the principles and objectives of this Directive, Member States may lay down particular provisions applicable to undertakings or establishments which pursue directly and essentially political, professional organisational, religious, charitable, educational, scientific or artistic aims, as well as aims involving information and the expression of opinions, on condition that, at the date of entry into force of this Directive, provisions of that nature already exist in national legislation.

3. Member States may derogate from this Directive through particular provisions applicable to the crews of vessels plying the high seas.

Article 4. Practical arrangements for information and consultation

1. In accordance with the principles set out in Article 1 and without prejudice to any provisions and/or practices in force more favourable to employees, the Member States shall determine the practical arrangements for exercising the right to information and consultation at the appropriate level in accordance with this Article.

2. Information and consultation shall cover:

(a) information on the recent and probable development of the undertaking's or the establishment's activities and economic situation;

(b) information and consultation on the situation, structure and probable development of employment within the undertaking or establishment and on any anticipatory measures envisaged, in particular where there is a threat to employment;

(c) information and consultation on decisions likely to lead to substantial changes in work organisation or in contractual relations, including those covered by the Community provisions referred to in Article 9(1).

3. Information shall be given at such time, in such fashion and with such content as are appropriate to enable, in particular, employees' representatives to conduct an adequate study and, where necessary, prepare for consultation.

4. Consultation shall take place:

(a) while ensuring that the timing, method and content thereof are appropriate;
(b) at the relevant level of management and representation, depending on the subject under discussion;
(c) on the basis of information supplied by the employer in accordance with Article 2(f) and of the opinion which the employees' representatives are entitled to formulate;
(d) in such a way as to enable employees' representatives to meet the employer and obtain a response, and the reasons for that response, to any opinion they might formulate;
(e) with a view to reaching an agreement on decisions within the scope of the employer's powers referred to in paragraph 2(c).

Article 5. Information and consultation deriving from an agreement

Member States may entrust management and labour at the appropriate level, including at undertaking or establishment level, with defining freely and at any time through negotiated agreement the practical arrangements for informing and consulting employees. These agreements, and agreements existing on the date laid down in Article 11, as well as any subsequent renewals of such agreements, may establish, while respecting the principles set out in Article 1 and subject to conditions and limitations laid down by the Member States, provisions which are different from those referred to in Article 4.

Article 6. Confidential information

1. Member States shall provide that, within the conditions and limits laid down by national legislation, the employees' representatives, and any experts who assist them, are not authorised to reveal to employees or to third parties, any information which, in the legitimate interest of the undertaking or establishment, has expressly been provided to them in confidence. This obligation shall continue to apply, wherever the said representatives or experts are, even after expiry of their terms of office. However, a Member State may authorise the employees' representatives and anyone assisting them to pass on confidential information to employees and to third parties bound by an obligation of confidentiality.

2. Member States shall provide, in specific cases and within the conditions and limits laid down by national legislation, that the employer is not obliged to communicate information or undertake consultation when the nature of that information or consultation is such that, according to objective criteria,

it would seriously harm the functioning of the undertaking or establishment or would be prejudicial to it.

3. Without prejudice to existing national procedures, Member States shall provide for administrative or judicial review procedures for the case where the employer requires confidentiality or does not provide the information in accordance with paragraphs 1 and 2. They may also provide for procedures intended to safeguard the confidentiality of the information in question.

Article 7. Protection of employees' representatives

Member States shall ensure that employees' representatives, when carrying out their functions, enjoy adequate protection and guarantees to enable them to perform properly the duties which have been assigned to them.

Article 8. Protection of rights

1. Member States shall provide for appropriate measures in the event of non-compliance with this Directive by the employer or the employees' representatives. In particular, they shall ensure that adequate administrative or judicial procedures are available to enable the obligations deriving from this Directive to be enforced.

2. Member States shall provide for adequate sanctions to be applicable in the event of infringement of this Directive by the employer or the employees' representatives. These sanctions must be effective, proportionate and dissuasive.

Article 9. Link between this Directive and other Community and national provisions

1. This Directive shall be without prejudice to the specific information and consultation procedures set out in Article 2 of Directive 98/59/EC and Article 7 of Directive 2001/23/EC.

2. This Directive shall be without prejudice to provisions adopted in accordance with Directives 94/45/EC and 98/74/EC.

3. This Directive shall be without prejudice to other rights to information, consultation and participation under national law.

4. Implementation of this Directive shall not be sufficient grounds for any regression in relation to the situation which already prevails in each Member State and in relation to the general level of protection of workers in the areas to which it applies.

Article 10. Transitional provisions

Notwithstanding Article 3, a Member State in which there is, at the date of entry into force of this Directive, no general, permanent and statutory system of information and consultation of employees, nor a general, permanent and statutory system of employee representation at the workplace allowing employees to be represented for that purpose, may limit the application of the national provisions implementing this Directive to:

(a) undertakings employing at least 150 employees or establishments employing at least 100 employees until 23 March 2007, and

(b) undertakings employing at least 100 employees or establishments employing at least 50 employees during the year following the date in point (a).

Article 11. Transposition

1. Member States shall adopt the laws, regulations and administrative provisions necessary to comply with this Directive not later than 23 March 2005 or shall ensure that management and labour introduce by that date the required provisions by way of agreement, the Member States being obliged to take all necessary steps enabling them to guarantee the results imposed by this Directive at all times. They shall forthwith inform the Commission thereof.

2. Where Member States adopt these measures, they shall contain a reference to this Directive or shall be accompanied by such reference on the occasion of their official publication. The methods of making such reference shall be laid down by the Member States.

Article 12. Review by the Commission

Not later than 23 March 2007, the Commission shall, in consultation with the Member States and the social partners at Community level, review the application of this Directive with a view to proposing any necessary amendments.

Article 13. Entry into force

This Directive shall enter into force on the day of its publication in the *Official Journal of the European Communities*.

Article 14. Addresses

This Directive is addressed to the Member States.

Done at Brussels, 11 March 2002.

For the European Parliament	*For the Council*
The President	*The President*
P. COX	J. PIQUÉ I CAMPS

Transfer of Undertakings (Protection of Employment) Regulations 1981 (SI 1981/1794) [as amended]

1 Citation, commencement and extent

(1) These Regulations may be cited as the Transfer of Undertakings (Protection of Employment) Regulations 1981.

(2) These Regulations, except Regulations 4 to 9 and 14, shall come into operation on 1st February 1982 and Regulations 4 to 9 and 14 shall come into operation on 1st May 1982.

(3) These Regulations, except Regulations 11(10) and 13(3) and (4), extend to Northern Ireland.

2 Interpretation

(1) In these Regulations–

'collective agreement', 'employers' association', and 'trade union' have the same meanings respectively as in the 1974 Act or, in Northern Ireland, the 1976 Order;

'collective bargaining' has the same meaning as it has in the 1975 Act or, in Northern Ireland, the 1976 Order;

'contract of employment' means any agreement between an employee and his employer determining the terms and conditions of his employment;

'employee' means any individual who works for another person whether under a contract of service or apprenticeship or otherwise but does not include anyone who provides services under a contract for services and references to a person's employer shall be construed accordingly;

'the 1974 Act', 'the 1975 Act', 'the 1978 Act' and 'the 1976 Order' mean, respectively, the Trade Union and Labour Relations Act 1974, the Employment Protection Act 1975, the Employment Protection (Consolidation) Act 1978 and the Industrial Relations (Northern Ireland) Order 1976;

'recognised', in relation to a trade union, means recognised to any extent by an employer, or two or more associated employers, (within the meaning of the 1978 Act, or, in Northern Ireland, the

1976 Order), for the purpose of collective bargaining;
'relevant transfer' means a transfer to which these regulations apply and 'transferor' and 'transferee' shall be construed accordingly; and
'undertaking' includes any trade or business . . .

(2) References in these Regulations to the transfer of part of an undertaking are references to a transfer of a part which is being transferred as a business and, accordingly, do not include references to a transfer of a ship without more.

(3) For the purposes of these Regulations the representative of a trade union recognised by an employer is an official or other person authorised to carry on collective bargaining with that employer by that union.

3 A relevant transfer

(1) Subject to the provisions of these Regulations, these Regulations apply to a transfer from one person to another of an undertaking situated immediately before the transfer in the United Kingdom or a part of one which is so situated.

(2) Subject as aforesaid, these Regulations so apply whether the transfer is effected by sale or by some other disposition or by operation of law.

(3) Subject as aforesaid, these Regulations so apply notwithstanding–

(a) that the transfer is governed or effected by the law of a country or territory outside the United Kingdom;
(b) that persons employed in the undertakings or part transferred ordinarily work outside the United Kingdom;
(c) that the employment of any of those persons is governed by any such law.

(4) It is hereby declared that a transfer of an undertaking or part of one–

(a) may be effected by a series of two or more transactions; and
(b) may take place whether or not any property is transferred to the transferee by the transferor.

(5) Where, in consequence (whether directly or indirectly) of the transfer of an undertaking or part of one which was situated immediately before the transfer in the United Kingdom, a ship within the meaning of the Merchant Shipping Act 1894 registered in the United Kingdom ceases to be so registered, these regulations shall not affect the right conferred by section 5 of the Merchant Shipping Act 1970 (right of seamen to be discharged when ship ceases to be registered in the United Kingdom) on a seaman employed in the ship.

4 Transfers by receivers and liquidators

(1) Where the receiver of the property of part or the property of a company or the administrator of a company appointed under Part II of the Insolvency Act 1986 or, in the case of a creditors' voluntary winding up, the liquidator of a company transfers the company's undertaking, or part of the company's undertaking (the 'relevant undertaking') to a wholly owned subsidiary of the company, the transfer shall for the purposes of these Regulations be deemed not to have been effected until immediately before–

    (a) the transferee company ceases (otherwise than by reason of its being wound up) to be a wholly owned subsidiary of the transferor company; or

    (b) the relevant undertaking is transferred by the transferee company to another person;

whichever first occurs, and, for the purposes of these Regulations, the transfer of the relevant undertaking shall be taken to have been effected immediately before that date by one transaction only.

(2) In this Regulation–

    'creditors' voluntary winding up' has the same meaning as in the Companies Act 1948 or, in Northern Ireland, the Companies Act (Northern Ireland) 1960; and

    'wholly owned subsidiary' has the same meaning as it has for the purposes of section 150 of the Companies Act 1948 and section 144 of the Companies Act (Northern Ireland) 1960.

5 Effect of relevant transfer on contracts of employment, etc

(1) Except where objection is made under paragraph (4A) below, a relevant transfer shall not operate so as to terminate the contract of employment of any person employed by the transferor in the undertaking or part transferred but any such contract which would otherwise have been terminated by the transfer shall have effect after the transfer as if originally made between the person so employed and the transferee.

(2) Without prejudice to paragraph (1) above but subject to paragraph (4A) below, on the completion of a relevant transfer–

    (a) all the transferor's rights, powers, duties and liabilities under or in connection with any such contract shall be transferred by virtue of this Regulation to the transferee; and

    (b) anything done before the transfer is completed by or in relation to the transferor in respect of that contract or a person employed in that undertaking or part shall be deemed to have been done by or in relation to the transferee.

(3) Any reference in paragraph (1) to (2) above to a person employed in an undertaking or part of one transferred by a relevant transfer is a

reference to a person so employed immediately before the transfer, including, where the transfer is effected by a series of two or more transactions, a person so employed immediately before any of those transactions.

(4) Paragraph (2) above shall not transfer or otherwise affect the liability of any person to be prosecuted for, convicted of and sentenced for any offence.

(4A) Paragraphs (1) and (2) above shall not operate to transfer his contract of employment and the rights, powers, duties and liabilities under or in connection with it if the employee informs the transferor or the transferee that he objects to becoming employed by the transferee.

(4B) Where an employee so objects the transfer of the undertaking or part in which he is employed shall operate so as to terminate his contract of employment with the transferor but he shall not be treated, for any purpose, as having been dismissed by the transferor.

(5) Paragraphs (1) and (4A) above are without prejudice to any right of an employee arising apart from these Regulations to terminate his contract of employment without notice if a substantial change is made in his working conditions to his detriment; but no such right shall arise by reason only that, under that paragraph, the identity of his employer changes unless the employee shows that, in all the circumstances, the change is a significant change and is to his detriment.

6 Effect of relevant transfer on collective agreements

Where at the time of a relevant transfer there exists a collective agreement made by or on behalf of the transferor with a trade union recognised by the transferor in respect of any employee whose contract of employment is preserved by Regulation 5(1) above, then–

  (a) without prejudice to section 18 of the 1974 Act or Article 63 of the 1976 Order (collective agreements presumed to be unenforceable in specified circumstances) that agreement, in its application in relation to the employee, shall, after the transfer, have effect as if made by or on behalf of the transferee with that trade union, and accordingly anything done under or in connection with it, in its application as aforesaid, by or in relation to the transferor before the transfer, shall, after the transfer, be deemed to have been done by or in relation to the transferee; and

  (b) any order made in respect of that agreement, in its application in relation to the employee, shall, after the transfer, have effect as if the transferee were a party to the agreement.

7 Exclusion of occupational pensions schemes

(1) Regulations 5 and 6 above shall not apply–

  (a) to so much of a contract of employment or collective agreement as relates to an occupational pension scheme within the meaning of the Social Security Pensions Act 1975 or the Social Security Pensions (Northern Ireland) Order 1975; or

(b) to any rights, powers, duties or liabilities under or in connection with any such contract of subsisting by virtue of any such agreement and relating to such a scheme or otherwise arising in connection with that person's employment and relating to such a scheme.

(2) For the purposes of paragraph (1) above any provisions of an occupational pension scheme which do not relate to benefits for old age, invalidity or survivors shall be treated as not being part of the scheme.

8 Dismissal of employee because of relevant transfer

(1) Where either before or after a relevant transfer, any employee of the transferor or transferee is dismissed, that employee shall be treated for the purposes of Part V of the 1978 Act and Articles 20 to 41 of the 1976 Order (unfair dismissal) as unfairly dismissed if the transfer or a reason connected with it is the reason or principal reason for his dismissal.

(2) Where an economic, technical or organisational reason entailing changes in the workforce of either the transferor or the transferee before or after a relevant transfer is the reason or principal reason for dismissing an employee–

(a) paragraph (1) above shall not apply to his dismissal; but

(b) without prejudice to the application of section 57(3) of the 1978 Act or Article 22(10) of the 1976 Order (test of fair dismissal), the dismissal shall for the purposes of section 57(1)(b) of that Act and Article 22(1)(b) of that Order (substantial reason for dismissal) be regarded as having been for a substantial reason of a kind such as to justify the dismissal of an employee holding the position which that employee held.

(3) The provisions of this Regulation apply whether or not the employee in question is employed in the undertaking or part of the undertaking transferred or to be transferred.

(4) Paragraph (1) above shall not apply in relation to the dismissal of any employee which was required by reason of the application of section 5 of the Aliens Restriction (Amendment) Act 1919 to his employment.

(5) Paragraph (1) above shall not apply in relation to a dismissal of an employee if–

(a) the application of section 54 of the 1978 Act to the dismissal of the employee is excluded by or under any provision of Part V or sections 141 to 149 of the 1978 Act or of section 237 or 238 of the Trade Union and Labour Relations (Consolidation) Act 1992; or

(b) the application of Article 20 of the 1976 Order to the dismissal of the employee is excluded by or under any provision of Part III or Article 76 of that Order.

9 Effect of relevant transfer on trade union recognition

(1) This Regulation applies where after a relevant transfer the undertaking or part of the undertaking transferred maintains an identity distinct from the remainder of the transferee's undertaking.

(2) Where before such a transfer an independent trade union is recognised to any extent by the transferor in respect of employees of any description who in consequence of the transfer become employees of the transferee, then, after the transfer—

(a) the union shall be deemed to have been recognised by the transferee to the same extent in respect of employees of that description so employed; and

(b) any agreement for recognition may be varied or rescinded accordingly.

10 Duty to inform and consult representatives

(1) In this Regulation and Regulation 11 below references to affected employees, in relation to a relevant transfer, are to any employees of the transferor or the transferee (whether or not employed in the undertaking or the part of the undertaking to be transferred) who may be affected by the transfer or may be affected by measures taken in connection with it; and references to the employer shall be construed accordingly.

(2) Long enough before a relevant transfer to enable the employer of any affected employees to consult all the persons who are appropriate representatives of any of those affected employees, the employer shall inform those representatives of—

(a) the fact that the relevant transfer is to take place, when, approximately, it is to take place and the reasons for it; and

(b) the legal, economic and social implications of the transfer for the affected employees; and

(c) the measures which he envisages he will, in connection with the transfer, take in relation to those employees or, if he envisages that no measures will be so taken, that fact; and

(d) if the employer is the transferor, the measures which the transferee envisages he will, in connection with the transfer, take in relation to such of those employees as, by virtue of Regulation 5 above, become employees of the transferee after the transfer or, if he envisages that no measures will be so taken, that fact.

(2A) For the purposes of this Regulation the appropriate representatives of any employees are—

(a) if the employees are of a description in respect of which an independent trade union is recognised by their employer, representatives of the trade union, or

(b)   in any other case, whichever of the following employee representatives the employer chooses:–

    (i)   employee representatives appointed or elected by the affected employees otherwise than for the purposes of this Regulation, who (having regard to the purposes for and the method by which they were appointed or elected) have authority from those employees to receive information and to be consulted about the transfer on their behalf;

    (ii)   employee representatives elected by them, for the purposes of this Regulation, in an election satisfying the requirements of Regulation 10A(1).

(3) The transferee shall give the transferor such information at such a time as will enable the transferor to perform the duty imposed on him by virtue of paragraph (2)(d) above.

(4) The information which is to be given to the appropriate representatives shall be given to each of them by being delivered to them, or sent by post to an address notified by them to the employer, or (in the case of representatives of a trade union) sent by post to the union at the address of its head or main office.

(5) Where an employer of any affected employees envisages that he will, in connection with the transfer, be taking measures in relation to any such employees he shall consult all the persons who are appropriate representatives of any of the affected employees in relation to whom he envisages taking measures with a view to seeking their agreement to measures to be taken.

(6) In the course of those consultations the employer shall–

(a)   consider any representations made by the appropriate representatives; and

(b)   reply to those representatives and, if he rejects any of those representations, state his reasons.

(6A) The employer shall allow the appropriate representatives access to the affected employees and shall afford to those representatives such accommodation and other facilities as may be appropriate.

(7) If in any case there are special circumstances which render it not reasonably practicable for an employer to perform a duty imposed on him by any of paragraphs (2) to (6), he shall take all such steps towards performing that duty as are reasonably practicable in the circumstances.

(8) Where–

(a)   the employer has invited any of the affected employees to elect employee representatives, and

(b)   the invitation was issued long enough before the time when the employer is required to give information under paragraph (2) above to allow them to elect representatives by that time, the employer shall be treated as complying with the requirements of this Regulation in relation to those employees if he complies with those requirements as soon as is reasonably practicable after the election of the representatives.

(8A) If, after the employer has invited affected employees to elect representatives, they fail to do so within a reasonable time, he shall give to each affected employee the information set out in paragraph (2).

10A

(1) The requirements for the election of employee representatives under Regulation 10(2A) are that–

    (a)   the employer shall make such arrangements as are reasonably practical to ensure that the election is fair;

    (b)   the employer shall determine the number of representatives to be elected so that there are sufficient representatives to represent the interests of all the affected employees having regard to the number and classes of those employees;

    (c)   the employer shall determine whether the affected employees should be represented either by representatives of all the affected employees or by representatives of particular classes of those employees;

    (d)   before the election the employer shall determine the term of office as employee representatives so that it is of sufficient length to enable information to be given and consultations under Regulation 10 to be completed;

    (e)   the candidates for election as employee representatives are affected employees on the date of the election;

    (f)   no affected employee is unreasonably excluded from standing for election;

    (g)   all affected employees on the date of the election are entitled to vote for employee representatives;

    (h)   the employees entitled to vote may vote for as many candidates as there are representatives to be elected to represent them or, if there are to be representatives for particular classes of employees, may vote for as many candidates as there are representatives to be elected to represent their particular class of employee;

    (i)   the election is conducted so as to secure that–

        (i)   so far as is reasonably practicable, those voting do so in secret, and

        (ii)   the votes given at the election are accurately counted.

(2) Where, after an election of employee representatives satisfying the requirements of paragraph (1) has been held, one of those elected ceases to act as an employee representative and any of those employees are no

longer represented, those employees shall elect another representative by an election satisfying the requirements of paragraph (1)(a), (e), (f) and (i).

11 Failure to inform or consult

(1) Where an employer has failed to comply with a requirement of Regulation 10 or Regulation 10A, a complaint may be presented to an employment tribunal on that ground–

(a) in the case of a failure relating to the election of employee representatives, by any of his employees who are affected employees;

(b) in the case of any other failure relating to employee representatives, by any of the employee representatives to whom the failure related,

(c) in the case of failure relating to representatives of a trade union, by the trade union, and

(d) in any other case, by any of his employees who are affected employees.

(2) If on a complaint under paragraph (1) above a question arises whether or not it was reasonably practicable for an employer to perform a particular duty or what steps he took towards performing it, it shall be for him to show–

(a) that there were special circumstances which rendered it not reasonably practicable for him to perform the duty; and

(b) that he took all such steps towards its performance as were reasonably practicable in those circumstances.

(2A) If on a complaint under paragraph (1) a question arises as to whether or not any employee representative was an appropriate representative for the purposes of Regulation 10, it shall be for the employer to show that the employee representative had the necessary authority to represent the affected employees.

(2B) On a complaint under sub-paragraph (1)(a) it shall be for the employer to show that the requirements in Regulation 10A have been satisfied.

(3) On any such complaint against a transferor that he had failed to perform the duty imposed upon him by virtue of paragraph (2)(d) or, so far as relating thereto, paragraph (7) of Regulation 10 above, he may not show that it was not reasonably practicable for him to perform the duty in question for the reason that the transferee had failed to give him the requisite information at the requisite time in accordance with Regulation 10(3) above unless he gives the transferee notice of his intention to show that fact; and the giving of the notice shall make the transferee a party to the proceedings.

(4) Where the tribunal finds a complaint under paragraph (1) above well-founded it shall make a declaration to that effect and may–

(a) order the employer to pay appropriate compensation to such descriptions of affected employees as may be specified in the award; or

(b) if the complaint is that the transferor did not perform the duty mentioned in paragraph (3) above and the transferor (after giving due notice) shows the facts so mentioned, order the transferee to pay appropriate compensation to such descriptions of affected employees as may be specified in the award.

(5) An employee may present a complaint to an employment tribunal on the ground that he is an employee of a description to which an order under paragraph (4) above relates and that the transferor or the transferee has failed, wholly or in part, to pay him compensation in pursuance of the order.

(6) Where the tribunal finds a complaint under paragraph (5) above well-founded it shall order the employer to pay the complainant the amount of compensation which it finds is due to him.

(7) . . .

(8) An employment tribunal shall not consider a complaint under paragraph (1) or (5) above unless it is presented to the tribunal before the end of the period of three months beginning with—

(a) the date on which the relevant transfer is completed, in the case of a complaint under paragraph (1);

(b) the date of the tribunal's order under paragraph (4) above, in the case of a complaint under paragraph (5);

or within such further period as the tribunal considers reasonable in a case where it is satisfied that it was not reasonably practicable for the complaint to be presented before the end of the period of three months.

(9) Section 129 of the 1978 Act (complaint to be sole remedy for breach of relevant rights) and section 133 of that Act (functions of conciliation officer) and Articles 58(2) and 62 of the 1977 Order (which make corresponding provision for Northern Ireland) shall apply to the rights conferred by this Regulation and to proceedings under this Regulation as they apply to the rights conferred by that Act or that Order and the employment tribunal proceedings mentioned therein.

(10) An appeal shall lie and shall lie only to the Employment Appeal Tribunal on a question of law arising from any decision of, or arising in any proceedings before, an [employment tribunal] under or by virtue of these Regulations; and section 13(1) of the Tribunals and Inquiries Act 1971 (appeal from certain tribunals to the High Court) shall not apply in relation to any such proceedings.

(11) In this Regulation 'appropriate compensation' means such sum not exceeding thirteen weeks' pay for the employee in question as the tribunal considers just and equitable having regard to the seriousness of the failure of the employer to comply with his duty.

(12) Schedule 14 to the 1978 Act or, in Northern Ireland, Schedule 2 to the 1976 Order shall apply for calculating the amount of a week's pay for any employee for the purposes of paragraph (11) above; and, for the purposes of that calculation, the calculation date shall be–

(a) in the case of an employee who is dismissed by reason of redundancy (within the meaning of section 81 of the 1978 Act or, in Northern Ireland, section 11 of the Contracts of Employment and Redundancy Payments Act (Northern Ireland) 1965) the date which is the calculation date for the purposes of any entitlement of his to a redundancy payment (within the meaning of that section) or which would be that calculation date if he were so entitled;

(b) in the case of an employee who is dismissed for any other reason, the effective date of termination (within the meaning of section 55 of the 1978 Act or, in Northern Ireland, Article 21 of the 1976 Order) of his contract of employment;

(c) in any other case, the date of the transfer in question.

11A Construction of references to employee representatives

For the purposes of Regulations 10 and 11 above persons are employee representatives if–

(a) they have been elected by employees for the specific purpose of being given information and consulted by their employer under Regulation 10 above; or

(b) having been elected [or appointed] by employees otherwise than for that specific purpose, it is appropriate (having regard to the purposes for which they were elected) for their employer to inform and consult them under that Regulation,

and (in either case) they are employed by the employer at the time when they are elected or appointed.

12 Restriction on contracting out

Any provision of any agreement (whether a contract of employment or not) shall be void in so far as it purports to exclude or limit the operation of Regulation 5, 8 or 10 above or the preclude any person from presenting a complaint to an employment tribunal under Regulation 11 above.

13 Exclusion of employment abroad or as dock worker

(1) Regulations 8, 10 and 11 of these Regulations do not apply to employment where under his contract of employment the employee ordinarily works outside the United Kingdom.

(2) For the purposes of this Regulation a person employed to work on board a ship registered in the United Kingdom shall, unless–

(a)   the employment is wholly outside the United Kingdom, or

(b)   he is not ordinarily resident in the United Kingdom.

be regarded as a person who under his contract ordinarily works in the United Kingdom.

(3), (4)   . . .

14

(Para (1), which amended the Employment Protection (Consolidation) Act 1978, s 4(4), became spent on the partial repeal of that subsection by the Employment Act 1982, s 21, Sch 4; para (2) applies to Northern Ireland.)

Public consultation document: government proposals for reform

TRANSFER OF UNDERTAKINGS (PROTECTION OF EMPLOYMENT) REGULATIONS 1981 (TUPE): GOVERNMENT PROPOSALS FOR REFORM

Introduction

1. Changes in the ownership of businesses and in service contracting are a normal part of business life in both the private sector and the public. Such changes can be made easier for all concerned if the employees know where they stand. The Transfer of Undertakings (Protection of Employment) Regulations 1981 (as amended) – commonly known as the TUPE Regulations – safeguard employees' rights where businesses change hands between employers. However, they are widely regarded, by all groups whose interests are affected by them, as operating less satisfactorily than they might. This can hamper necessary change, and impose a burden on business. This consultation document sets out proposals for the Regulations' reform. A more detailed background paper on the proposals, including a Regulatory Impact Assessment, is also available.

2. Responses should be sent by 15 December 2001 to:

Mrs Pat Wright
Employment Relations Directorate
Department of Trade and Industry
UG067
1 Victoria Street
London SW1H 0ET

or by e-mail to pat.wright@dti.gov.uk.

Further copies of this document, and copies of *the more detailed background paper* (180Kb), can be obtained from the Employment Relations website or from the DTI publications order line at EC Logistics by telephoning 0870 1502 500 or faxing 0870 1502 333.

For information on consultation on the TUPE Regulations in Northern Ireland, please contact William Caldwell at:

Employment Rights and New Deal
Room 301
Adelaide House
Adelaide Street
Belfast BT2 8FD

Comments

If you would like to comment on the way this consultation is being handled (as opposed to the proposals it outlines), please write to the DTI consultation co-ordinator, Andrew Dobbie, at:

Departmental Regulatory Impact Unit,
Department of Trade and Industry
1 Victoria Street
London SW1H 0ET

Versions of this document in Welsh or large print or on tape

A Welsh language summary of this document is available from Mrs Pat Wright at the address above. We can also provide large print and taped versions of the consultation document on request – please contact Mrs Pat Wright for these.

This consultation complies with the criteria of the Government's new Code of Practice on written consultation. A list of these criteria can be found in the Annex to this document.

Background

3. The TUPE Regulations were originally introduced in order to implement the EC Acquired Rights Directive (sometimes known as the Business Transfers Directive), adopted in 1977. They are designed to safeguard employees' rights when the business in which they work changes hands between employers. The Directive was revised in 1998, and a consolidated version adopted in 2001. The main impact of the 1998 revision was to give Member States a number of new optional flexibilities to tailor their implementing measures to national circumstances. These flexibilities, and the extent to which the Government proposes to take advantage of them, are described below.

Proposals

General objectives

4. The Government considers that the TUPE Regulations are based on a positive principle – the coupling of flexibility for business with fairness for employees. If made to work effectively, they should assist the smooth management of necessary change, in both the private sector and the public, by

giving assurance to and securing the commitment of the employees affected. The Government's aim in reforming the Regulations is to ensure that they operate as effectively as possible for all those whose interests depend on them.

Scope

5. The scope of the legislation is the most extensively debated and litigated aspect of the current Regulations. Ideally, everyone should know where they stand, so employers can plan effectively in a climate of fair competition and affected employees are appropriately protected as a matter of course. In the past, however, this has not always been the case.

   6. The revised Directive gives for the first time an explicit definition of a transfer of an undertaking, intended to clarify the existing legal position without changing it. The Government proposes essentially to adopt this definition in the new Regulations. This alone, however, may be insufficient to address the problems that have arisen. The Government considers that there may be a case for taking further measures in two particular areas – transfers within public administration, and service provision changes – that have in the past been particularly frequent sources of confusion and dispute.

TRANSFERS WITHIN PUBLIC ADMINISTRATION

7. **The Government proposes to address the issue of transfers within public administration through:**

- **applying the Cabinet Office Statement of Practice** *Staff Transfers in the Public Sector* **(issued in January 2000); and**
- **where appropriate, and subject to prior consultation with interested parties, ensuring that TUPE-equivalent protections are afforded to affected employees:**

  - **in case-specific legislation, where that is the vehicle for effecting a particular transfer within public administration; or**
  - **by regulations under section 38 of the Employment Relations Act 1999[1] on an** *ad hoc* **basis in other cases or classes of cases outside the Directive's scope.**

   8. Copies of *Staff Transfers in the Public Sector* are obtainable by telephone from 020 7276 1638, by e-mail request from pgreasley@cabinet-office.x.gsi.gov.uk or from the website http://www.cabinet-office.gov.uk.

SERVICE PROVISION CHANGES

9. There has in the past been uncertainty over the Regulations' application in cases where a service is 'contracted-out' or 'outsourced', or a service contract is re-let to a new contractor, or a previously contracted-for service is taken in-house or 'contracted-in'. For convenience, all these types of

changes are referred to below as 'service provision changes', and the party on behalf of whom the service activities are performed as the 'client'.

10. It is well established that the Regulations can in principle apply in relation to service provision changes. Whether or not any such change does constitute a relevant transfer of an undertaking depends on all the factual circumstances. The key question is whether or not there is a transfer of (in the words of the Directive) 'an economic entity' – i.e. 'an organised grouping of resources which has the objective of pursuing an economic activity' – that 'retains its identity' in the process. The difficulty of answering this question in service provision change cases is the root cause of most of the problems that have arisen in this regard in the past.

11. **The Government would welcome views on whether or not additional measures, going beyond the requirements of the Directive, should be taken in the Regulations in relation to service provision changes, and if so what form these should take. Views are also invited on whether there should be:**

(a) **separate legislative or administrative measures introduced by individual government departments specifically for the parts of the public sector within their responsibility, underpinning the policy in *Staff Transfers in the Public Sector*; or**

(b) **a general extension of the Regulations' scope in relation to service provision changes for public and private sectors alike using the powers in section 38 of the 1999 Act.**

12. A possible approach for taking forward the proposal at point (b) is set out and discussed in the *more detailed background paper* (180Kb) on the Government's proposals. (See paragraph 1 above.)

Occupational pensions

13. Rights, powers, duties and liabilities in respect of continuing membership of occupational pension schemes were excluded from the coverage of the original Directive and do not transfer under TUPE. Accrued rights in an occupational pension scheme are however covered by the Directive and are protected in the UK under pensions regulations. Where TUPE applies, therefore, the only rights excluded from the otherwise automatic transfer of employees' terms and conditions are rights to continuing active membership of an occupational pension scheme, where such rights existed prior to the transfer.

14. The Government's policy is that former public sector employees transferred to the private sector should continue to have pension provision made for them. The Government considers the current legal position is not certain and that there is at present a risk of claims of constructive dismissal where the transferor does not require the transferee to provide broadly comparable pension rights after the transfer. Central guidance to government departments and local authorities lays down that the transferee employer in transfers from such public sector bodies is generally required to offer trans-

ferred employees occupational pension provision 'broadly comparable' to that afforded by the transferor. Whether or not the 'broadly comparable' condition is met in any particular case is assessed according to established criteria by the Government Actuary's Department (GAD). The Treasury has reaffirmed this policy in a note entitled *Staff Transfers from Central Government: A Fair Deal for Staff Pensions,* and GAD has set out its approach in a Statement of Practice entitled *Assessment of Broad Comparability of Pension Rights.* The legal position has never been directly tested in the courts, however, and the risk of successful legal challenge has apparently been widely discounted in the private sector. In this one respect of pension terms, therefore, private sector employees, unlike public sector employees, may still in practice find themselves in a significantly worse position after a transfer than they were before it.

15. **The Government considers that the uncertain legal position is unsatisfactory, and that in implementing the Directive legal certainty should be achieved. There are a number of possible ways in which this could be done. One would be simply to provide that ongoing occupational pension rights are not transferred to the transferee, extinguishing any arguments along the lines discussed above. The Government is not attracted to this, however. Other possible approaches would be:**

(a) **amending the TUPE Regulations so as to provide that ongoing occupational pension rights are not transferred to the transferee, but preserving the current public sector policy by way of separate legislative or administrative measures introduced by individual government departments specifically for the parts of the public sector for which they are responsible; or**

(b) **amending the TUPE Regulations to provide a degree of protection for occupational pension rights on transfer, for public and private sector employees alike.**

The Government would welcome views on this issue.

16. If the approach described at point (b) above were to be taken, the Government would aim to strike a balance between protecting transferred employees and minimising additional burdens on private sector employers. A number of options for meeting this objective are set out in the more detailed background paper on the Government's proposals. They would of course apply only where the transferor provided an occupational pension for the employees in question to start with, so that the transferee would not be required to set up an occupational pension scheme where the transferor did not provide such a scheme. The options may be summarised as follows:

Option 1: If the transferor offered either a contracted-out salary related scheme (COSR) or a contracted-out money purchase scheme (COMP), then the transferee would be required to offer a scheme of the same type meeting a certain minimum standard. If the transferor offered a contracted-in scheme, then the transferee would be required to offer some form of occupational pension scheme that was Revenue-approved but with no specified form or level of benefits.

Option 1a: As for option 1, except that there would be a limit placed on the reduction in benefits an employee could suffer.

Option 2: The transferee would still be required to offer a contracted-out occupational pension scheme if the transferor offered one, but could switch from COSR to COMP or *vice versa.* Contracted-in schemes would be dealt with as under Option 1.

Option 2a: This would incorporate a 'safety net' for employees analogous to that suggested in Option 1a.

Option 3: The transferee would be able to choose whether to offer a salary-related or a money purchase scheme, irrespective of the nature or level of benefits afforded by the transferor, provided that the scheme met a prescribed benchmark.

Option 4: There would be a requirement for the benefits under the transferee's scheme to be of a similar value to those under the transferor's scheme

The Government would welcome views on the relative merits of these options.

17. If one of these options were to be pursued, the Government would propose to provide also that transferees were permitted to pay transferred employees adequate alternative compensation in exceptional circumstances where it was not reasonably practicable for them to meet the new requirements.

THE *'FRANKLING'* CASE

18. In the *Frankling* case, the EAT found that certain age-related payments to which an employee would become entitled on redundancy under terms and conditions applicable in the NHS did not pass across in a TUPE transfer because the benefits in question:

- arose under legislation rather than under a contractual obligation on the employer to pay them to the employees; and
- fell within the occupational pensions exclusion in the Directive and TUPE.

The same issues have subsequently arisen in the *Beckman* case, and the High Court has referred them to the ECJ for a preliminary ruling.

19. **The Government's policy is that, whatever ruling the ECJ makes in the *Beckman* case, benefits of this kind should pass across in a TUPE transfer. It proposes to make specific provision to this effect in the amended Regulations.**

Notification of employee liability information

20. The revised Directive gives Member States a new option to introduce provisions requiring the transferor to notify the transferee of all the rights

and obligations in relation to employees that will be transferred – so far as those rights and obligations are or ought to be known to the transferor at the time of the transfer.

21. **The Government proposes to take advantage of this by providing that:**

- **the transferor in a prospective transfer of an undertaking is required to give the transferee written notification of all the rights and obligations in relation to employees that are to be transferred;**
- **if any of the rights or obligations in question change between the time that such notification of them is given and the completion of the transfer, the transferor is required to give the transferee written notification of the change;**
- **both these types of notification may be given in more than one instalment, but every instalment must be given:**

  - **in good time before the completion of the transfer; or**
  - **if special circumstances make this not reasonably practicable, as soon as is reasonably practicable and in any case no later than completion of the transfer.**

22. The question of possible remedies for breach of this new requirement is discussed in the *more detailed background paper* (180Kb) on the Government's proposals.

Dismissal by reason of a transfer of an undertaking

23. Regulation 8(1) of the current TUPE Regulations makes a dismissal automatically unfair under the unfair dismissal provisions of the Employment Rights Act 1996 (subject to the normal qualifying conditions, including one year's continuous employment) where 'the transfer or a reason connected with it is the reason or principal reason' for the dismissal. Regulation 8(2) then provides an exception from this general rule in those cases where 'an economic, technical or organisational reason entailing changes in the workforce' – generally referred to as an ETO reason – is 'the reason or principal reason' for the dismissal. In such cases the dismissal may be fair or unfair, depending on whether or not the employer has acted reasonably in treating that reason as sufficient to justify it.

24. The Government recognises that uncertainty has arisen about the interpretation of Regulation 8, leading to cases before the employment tribunals and the higher courts. A particular issue has arisen as to whether dismissals for a reason connected with the transfer – Regulation 8(1) – and dismissals for an ETO reason – Regulation 8(2) – are two mutually exclusive categories or whether the latter are a subset of the former. **The Government aims to improve the drafting of these provisions in the amended Regulations, in particular by making clear that ETO reasons are a subset of reasons connected with the transfer.**

Changes to the terms and conditions of employment of affected employees

25. There has also been some uncertainty as to the circumstances in which a change in the terms and conditions of employees affected by a transfer can be validly made. **The Government proposes to improve the operation of the Regulations by making clear that they do not preclude transfer-related changes to terms and conditions that are made for an ETO reason – that is, an 'economic, technical or organisational reason entailing changes in the workforce'.** The lawfulness of such changes will then clearly depend only on the normal considerations that would apply irrespective of a transfer.

Application of the legislation in relation to insolvency proceedings

26. Reflecting the position previously established in ECJ case law, the revised Directive provides that, unless Member States provide otherwise (which the Government does not propose to do), the normal safeguards for employees against transfer-related changes to terms and conditions and transfer-related dismissals do not apply where 'the transferor is the subject of bankruptcy proceedings or any analogous insolvency proceedings which have been instituted with a view to the liquidation of the assets of the transferor and are under the supervision of a competent public authority (which may be an insolvency practitioner authorised by a competent public authority).' Procedures for which the Insolvency Act 1986 provides that fall within this description in the UK include in particular compulsory winding-up and bankruptcy, and possibly also creditors' voluntary winding-up.

27. The revised Directive also gives Member States two new options in cases where its requirements apply in relation to 'insolvency proceedings . . . under the supervision of a competent public authority (which may be an insolvency practitioner determined by national law)'. Procedures that fall within this description in the UK include in particular administration, company and individual voluntary arrangements and creditors' voluntary winding-up, but not administrative receivership or any other receivership or members' voluntary winding-up.

28. The two new options are to provide that:

- in cases giving rise to protection for employees at least equivalent to that provided for in situations covered by the EC Insolvency Protection Directive (implemented in the UK by the insolvency payments provisions of the Employment Rights Act 1996), the transferor's pre-existing debts toward the employees do not pass to the transferee; and/or
- employers and employee representatives may, exceptionally, agree changes to terms and conditions of employment by reason of the transfer itself, provided that this is in accordance with national law and practice and with a view to ensuring the survival of the business and thereby preserving jobs.

29. The underlying aim of these options is to allow Member States to promote the sale of insolvent businesses as going concerns. This is in line with the 'rescue culture' which the Government wishes to promote.

30. **The benefits of exercising the first option are expected to outweigh the relatively modest additional 'deadweight' costs in insolvency payments from the National Insurance Fund (which would in any event be offset by other savings). The Government therefore proposes to provide that where insolvency proceedings within the new derogation have been opened in respect of a transferor, any outstanding debts toward employees either:**

* **fall to be met from the National Insurance Fund, if they are within the categories and statutory upper limits on amounts guaranteed under the insolvency payments provisions of the Employment Rights Act 1996; or**
* **pass to the transferee, as at present, if they are not.**

31. **The Government also proposes to take up the second option and provide that where insolvency proceedings falling within the new derogation have been opened in respect of a transferor, changes by reason of the transfer itself (i.e. changes for which there is no ETO reason that would render them potentially valid in any event) may be lawfully made to the terms and conditions of employment of affected employees if:**

* **they are agreed between either the transferor or the transferee and appropriate representatives of those employees;**
* **they are designed to safeguard employment opportunities by ensuring the survival of the undertaking or business or part of the undertaking or business; and**
* **they are not otherwise contrary to UK law (e.g. the National Minimum Wage Act).**

32. The definition of 'appropriate representatives' used for these purposes would be consistent with that used for information and consultation purposes (Regulation 10 of the current TUPE Regulations). **In cases involving non-union representatives, in order for the agreement to be effective in varying the contracts of employment of the individual employees represented, it would have to be in writing and the employer would have to have given the employees in question the text of it in advance of it coming into effect, along with such guidance as they might reasonably require in order to understand it fully. Representatives for the purposes of agreeing changes to terms and conditions would be given rights equivalent to those enjoyed by representatives for information and consultation purposes. Those who participate in the election of such representatives would also be given equivalent rights.**

HIVING DOWN

33. **The Government believes that in the light of case law developments, and of its proposal to take advantage of the new derogations in the Directive,**

the existing provision in Regulation 4 of TUPE relating to 'hiving down' no longer serves any useful purpose. It therefore proposes to remove that provision.

Continuity of employee representation

34. The revised Directive contains a requirement relating to continuity of employee representation in cases where a transferred undertaking retains its autonomy. **To make explicit that UK legislation is fully in line with this requirement, the Government proposes to provide expressly that the effect of union recognition declarations made by the Central Arbitration Committee (CAC) under the provisions introduced by the Employment Relations Act 1999 is appropriately preserved across a transfer.**

35. The revised Directive also contains a new provision relating to continuity of employee representation in a case where a transferred undertaking does not retain its autonomy. Such a situation might arise where, for instance, a small, independently managed business became – following a transfer – a department of a larger business with its own existing management structure. If the transferor and transferee had different employee representation arrangements – for instance, if the transferor recognised a union but the transferee did not – there might be a period of time following the transfer when the employees would lose their representation. **The Government would welcome views as to whether or not any new measures might usefully be introduced in the UK in the light of this new provision; and, if so, what form they might take.**

Information and consultation of employee representatives

36. The provisions on information and consultation of employee representatives in the revised Directive differ from those in the original Directive in three relatively minor respects. **The Government proposes to amend the Regulations to remove any possible doubt that they comply fully with the Directive's requirements in this regard.**

Employers' liability compulsory insurance

37. Private sector employers carrying on any business in the UK are legally obliged to insure themselves against liabilities to employees for bodily injury or disease arising from their employment. It has been established in case law that such liabilities automatically pass from the transferor to the transferee in a TUPE transfer. It has also been established that the benefit of the insurance cover bought by the transferor in compliance with the legal requirements similarly passes across in a transfer, so that the transferee is able to call on that cover to meet any such liabilities incurred while the business was in the hands of the transferor. The Government considers that this position is satisfactory as far as transfers between private sector employers are concerned. There remains however a problem as far as transfers from public sec-

tor employers to private sector employers are concerned: public sector employers are generally exempted from the requirement to effect insurance cover and, other than in exceptional cases where they have insured themselves on a voluntary basis, there is no cover to transfer.

38. **The Government therefore proposes to introduce provision for the transferor and transferee to be jointly and severally liable for liabilities to employees for injury or disease arising from their pre-transfer employment in those cases where the transferor was a public sector employer exempt from the legal insurance requirement.**

Territorial extent, etc.

39. The Government proposes to:

- **remove the current limitation of rights under the TUPE Regulations to employees who ordinarily work in the UK; but**
- **retain the effect of the current provision restricting seafarers' ability to qualify to cases where the ship on which they are employed is registered as belonging to a port in the UK, they are ordinarily resident in the UK and the work is not wholly outside the UK.**

40. This would bring the position into line with that under other aspects of the employment rights legislation, in relation to which similar amendments were made by the Employment Relations Act 1999. In future, whether or not an individual working outside the UK could potentially qualify for rights under the Regulations would depend (except in the case of seafarers) on the normal operation of international law.

Ships

41. Regulation 2(2) excludes 'the transfer of a ship without more' from the Regulations' coverage. 'Ship' has been interpreted in case law as meaning a ship and its crew. The Government considers that where there is a transfer between employers of a ship and its crew as part of a business, the Regulations do in principle apply. **As some uncertainty has arisen over this point, the Government proposes to amend the Regulations to make their intended meaning clear.**

ANNEX

Below are the consultation criteria outlined in the Government's new Code of Practice on consultation. These criteria have been followed in this document.

1. Timing of consultation should be built into the planning process for a policy (including legislation) or service from the start, so that it has the best prospect of improving the proposals concerned, and so that sufficient time is left for it at each stage.

2. It should be clear who is being consulted, about what questions, in what timescale and for what purpose.

3. A consultation document should be as simple and concise as possible. It should include a summary, in two pages at most, of the main questions it seeks views on. It should make it as easy as possible for readers to respond, make contact or complain.

4. Documents should be made widely available, with the fullest use of electronic means (though not to the exclusion of others) and effectively drawn to the attention of all interested groups and individuals.

5. Sufficient time should be allowed for considered responses from all groups with an interest. Twelve weeks should be the standard minimum period for a consultation.

6. Responses should be carefully and open-mindedly analysed, and the results made widely available, with an account of the views expressed, and the reasons for decisions finally taken.

7. Departments should monitor and evaluate consultations, designating a consultation co-ordinator who will ensure the lessons are disseminated.

Draft letters and forms

Letter no. 1: Letter to employers from the transferee informing them of their right to elect a representative

Dear [*name of employee*]

Re: Transfer of business from [*name of transferor*] to [*name of transferee*]

I am now able to confirm that the business will be transferring from ourselves to the transferee on [*date*].

This means that all employees will be automatically transferred to the transferee in accordance with the Transfer of Undertakings (Protection of Employment) Regulations 1981.

The transferor has assured us that all employees will transfer with the benefits of their continuous employment and with no changes to their existing contractual terms and conditions of employment.

Employees will not transfer with the benefit on non-contractual terms such as collectively agreed terms, or of disciplinary or grievance procedures. You will be informed of the new procedures that will apply after transfer during the consultation period which is a [*specify*] day period commencing on the [*date*]. Your pension rights do not transfer across with you.

It is important that all employees are fully consulted over this transfer and it is intended to use an elected body of colleagues for the purpose of group consultation. It is also our intention to use the shop stewards/local representatives of the recognised trade union, which is the [*name of trade union*].

Group consultation will include discussion of the time scales for the transfer, and any proposed changes in contractual and non-contractual terms and working practices. It will also offer you an opportunity to raise any concerns you have about the future of the business and your place within it both collectively and individually. There will also be individual consultations after the group consultation has been completed in order to address any particular concerns you may have about your career development, job security and the options available.

I would be grateful if you could complete and return the attached form and return it to the [*name of department*] by the [*date*].

If you have any queries please do not hesitate to contact [*name*].

Yours sincerely

Form no. 2: Group consultation nominations

In order for me to participate fully in the group consultation, I wish to propose that the following person(s) represent me in the elected consultation group:

	Yes	No
1. The recognised trade union representative	☐	☐

If no please provide an alternative name of an employee

2. Name ....

Signed: ....

Dated: ....

Name of employee ....

(Please return to Personnel by [date] at the latest.)

Form no. 3: Ballot form

Please find below the nominations for the election of representatives who have been proposed and are prepared to be involved in the group consultation process.

You may vote for a maximum of [*specify*] representatives by placing an (X) in the box.

By electing these representatives, you are giving them authority to receive information and be consulted on your behalf during the group consultation during the period of [*date*] to [*date*].

Please complete this form by putting an 'X' by a maximum of [*specify*] names and return it to the [*name of department*] by [*date*].

Spoilt ballot papers will be considered void.

Nominees

Name	**Vote**
....	☐
....	☐
....	☐
....	☐
....	☐
....	☐
....	☐
....	☐
....	☐

Signed .... Name of employee ....

Form no. 4: Consultation forms

First Group Meeting

- Date
- Attendees
- Minutes of meeting
- Documents supplied to consultation group by (i) transferor and (ii) transferee
- Date of second meeting

Signed: ....

Second Group Meeting

- Date
- Attendees
- Minutes of meeting
- Documents supplied to consultation group by (i) transferor and (ii) transferee
- Copies of correspondence between the transferor and transferee produced in connection with group consultations

Signed: ....

Date: ....

First Individual Meeting

- Date
- Name of employee
- Date of commencement of service, salary and contractual benefits, non-contractual terms
- Minutes of meeting

Signed [*Manager*] ....

[*Employee*] ....

Second Individual Meeting

- Date
- Name of employee
- Date of previous meeting
- Attached minutes
- Date minutes agreed
- Minutes of meeting

	Yes	No
Employee transferring	☐	☐

If no letter received from employee confirming objection to transfer [*letter 5*]

| Compromise agreement utilised | ☐ | ☐ |

Date: ....

Letter no. 5: Suggested letter to be signed by employees who wish to object to transferring

I have today discussed with [*name of manager*] of [*name of transferor*] the effect for me of the proposed transfer to [*name of transferee*] of the undertaking in which I am employed.

Having been informed that in law my contract of employment will transfer automatically to the new employer upon the transfer of the undertaking and that, if I refused to be employed by the new employer my employment will cease without my having any right to receive a redundancy payment or to claim unfair dismissal, I nevertheless hereby confirm my refusal to transfer.

I do this in the knowledge that my employment with [*name of transferor*] will immediately cease by reason of the transfer.

Letter no. 6: Suggested letter to be sent to employees just before the transfer

Dear [*name*]

[*date*]

I am writing to let you, as an employee of this organisation, know that negotiations for a change of ownership of the [*undertaking*] [*section*] [*unit*] in which you are employed have been taking place with [*specify*]. Our reasons for entering into these negotiations were [*specify*].

It is now expected that the formal transfer will take place on [*date*].

As this will be a transfer to which the Transfer of Undertakings (Protection of Employment) Regulations 1981 apply, I can now inform you that:

1. Your contract of employment will automatically transfer to the new employer, who will take on responsibility for it as if it had originally been entered into between you and him.

2. Your period of continuous service with [*the company, firm, organisation*] will count as continuous employment with the new employer, so any statutory employment rights dependent on length of service (e.g. the right to receive redundancy payment if you are made redundant after two years' continuous service with the same employer) will count in your employment with the new employer.

3. No measures will be taken by us to terminate your employment prior to the moment of transfer, and I understand from the new employer that he hopes you will continue in your job as his employee after the transfer goes through.

4. If before the date of the transfer you inform us as your present employer, or your new employer, that you object to becoming employed by the new employer, the effect in law will be that your contract of employment will be treated as being terminated by you because of the transfer and not for any reason as having been terminated by us.

Yours sincerely

Letter no. 7: Letter to employee from the transferee after the date of transfer

Dear [*name of employee*]

On [*date*] the business of [*the transferor*] was transferred to [*transferee*] in accordance with the provisions of the Transfer of Undertakings (Protection of Employment) Regulations 1981. As from the above date your new employer will be the transferee and all other terms and conditions of your employment remain the same save for:

1. [*List the terms and conditions of employment that will change as a result of the transfer*].

2. The benefit of any terms applicable to collectively agreed terms also do not transfer with your employment, as they are not contractual terms. The following terms will, therefore, no longer apply to your employment [*list terms*].

3. Nor does the benefit of any company pension scheme transfer, in accordance with reg. 7 of the Transfer of Undertakings (Protection of Employment) Regulations 1981. The transferee does/does not offer a company pension scheme (which you are invited to contribute to). Details are available from [*name*].

4. Details of the disciplinary and grievance procedure of the transferee are set out in the accompanying handbook [*or*: the statutory grievance procedure applies to your contract of employment (*this will be implied into all contracts of employment where there is no contractual scheme after April 2003*)].

It is confirmed that your period of continuous employment began on [*the date in your original contract of employment with the transferor*].

If you have any questions regarding the transfer please do not hesitate to contact [*name*].

Yours sincerely

Letter no. 8: Letter providing information to trade unions and inviting consultation on the transfer of an undertaking in accordance with the transfer of Undertakings (Protection of Employment) Regulations 1981

To [*e.g. local full-time official of recognised trade union*]

[*date*]

Dear [*insert name*]

I am writing to you in accordance with reg. 10 of the Transfer of Undertakings (Protection of Employment) Regulations 1981 (the regulations) to inform you of our proposal to transfer the business to [*name of transferee*].

It is proposed that the transfer of the business will take place on [*date*]. The reasons for the transfer are [*specify in detail the reason for the transfer with reference to any relevant documentation or evidence if appropriate*].

The proposed transfer will affect [*identify number and description of employees*] 'the affected employees' who are presently employed in the undertaking. The affected employees will, by virtue of the operation of the regulations, transfer on their existing terms and conditions of employment and with continuity of employment for statutory and contractual purposes. As there will be no changes to existing terms and conditions of employment [(*save in respect of pensions – see further below*)], it is not envisaged that there will be any economic implications arising from the transfer and nor are there any social implications.

It is not envisaged that we will be taking any measures in connection with the transfer in relation to those employees who will be affected by the transfer or [*specify any measures that may be taken, if any*].

Although in all other respects the terms and conditions of employment of those employees who will be transferring with the undertaking will be unaffected by the transfer of the undertaking, it will be necessary for their existing pension arrangements to be changed, since they will be unable to continue as members of the company pension scheme following the transfer. Arrangements will be implemented in relation to employees who are members of the company pension scheme to enable them to become members of the transferee's company pension scheme upon the transfer of their employment to [*transferee*]. The [*transferee*] pension scheme offers similar benefits to the [*transferor's*] pension scheme.

[*transferee*] has advised us that they do/do not envisage taking any other measures in relation to employees who transfer with the undertaking. The measures they envisage taking are [*specify*].

We would be pleased to meet with you on week beginning [*specify*] to discuss the proposed transfer of [*specify*] and to consult with you regarding any measures it is envisaged will be taken in connection with the transfer and to consider and reply to any representations which you wish to make on the subject of these measures.

197

May we suggest an explanatory meeting on [*date*] with any appointed officials, representatives from ourselves and for the transferee to agree on a mutually beneficial timetable to provide full information and consultation in accordance with reg. 10.

Yours sincerely

APPENDIX 6

Draft indemnity clause

1.1 The transferor and the transferee agree that not less than 28 days before the date of the transfer and during the relevant consultation period they will collectively consider their staffing requirements with the relevant appropriate representatives and will supply to them and to each other all of the consultation information. Both the transferor and the transferee will then consult with the relevant appropriate representatives when measures are to be taken in relation to any employee or objecting employee. Consultation will be undertaken with a view to seeking agreement to any measures to be taken.

1.2 When the consultation period has elapsed the transferor and the transferee will identify objecting employees and employees who wish to the transfer to the transferee.

1. The transferor will take such steps as are necessary to ensure that objecting employees are informed of the consequences of objecting to the transfer in writing 14 days before the transfer date.
2. The transferor will pay to each employee on or before the date of the transfer of his or her employment to the transferee all remuneration (including all emoluments, benefits, benefits in kind, bonuses and incentive payments) due or accrued up to the date of transfer of the employee's employment to the transferee.
3. The employees will transfer from the transferor to the transferee on the transfer date.

1.3 The transferor agrees to meet all costs of objecting employees which may arise as a consequence of any act or omission of the transferor including but not limited to any such costs, claim, liability, expense or demand relating to or arising out of:

(a) the transferor's rights, duties and/or liabilities under or in connection with any such contract of employment and any collective agreement (which rights, powers, duties and/or liabilities transfer to the transferee by virtue of the 1981 regulations and/or Directive);
(b) anything done or omitted to be done by or in relation to the transferor in respect of any such contract of employment and any such

collective agreement or otherwise in respect of any such employee which is deemed to have been done or omitted by or in relation to the transferee by virtue of the 1981 regulations;

(c) any claim by any appropriate representative of the transferor arising out of any failure or alleged failure by the transferor or any such third party to comply with any legal obligation to such appropriate representative whether under reg. 10 of the 1981 regulations or under the Directive and whether the claim arises before or after the transfer date;

(d) any claim by or liability to any such employee for any redundancy payment or compensation for wrongful dismissal or liability to reinstate or re-engage any such employee or for any additional award for failing to comply with any order to reinstate or re-engage any such employee or for any protective award or otherwise in connection with or arising out of the operation by the 1981 regulations and/or Directive in relation to any such employee;

(e) and including (but without limitation) all demands, actions, proceedings and any reasonable and proper legal costs or expenses which the transferee may incur in settling, contesting or otherwise dealing with any such liability claim or expenses or demand as aforesaid, provided that the indemnities for the benefit of the transferee under this clause shall not apply to the extent that any such cost, claim, liability, expense or demand or legal costs arising out of the transferee's failure to comply with its obligations under reg. 10 of the 1981 regulations or as a result of any other act or omission of the transferee.

1.4   Provided that the parties comply with clause 1.1 if as a result of the application of the 1981 regulations or the Directive, any contract of employment of any objecting employee has effect under the transfer as if originally made between the transferee and such objecting employee. The transferee may, within ten days of becoming aware of such fact, terminate the employment of the employee concerned, with or without notice and the transferor shall:

(a) indemnify the transferee against all costs, claims, liabilities, demands and expenses arising out of or in connection with such termination (including, for the avoidance of doubt, all legal costs and expenses and any statutory or other compensation or awards payable in consequences such as termination); and

(b) indemnify the transferee against all reasonable costs and expenses of employing such objecting employee from the date of the transfer until such termination.

1.5   The transferee and the transferor shall each use their respective reasonable endeavours to ensure that so far as it may be within their respective capabilities (but not so far as to oblige either party to offer or to continue employment) so to do any potential liability to any employee of the trans-feror which liability would or might be subject to the indemnity in clauses 1.2 and 1.3 above shall so far as may be reasonably practicable in the cir-cumstances of any particular case be avoided or minimised.

1.6　The transferor and the transferee may, during the consultation period, propose to the employees that their terms and conditions be har-monised after the transfer date with those terms and conditions offered by the transferee to their existing staff. The harmonisation of the terms and conditions of employment is to be effected by way of a compromise agreement.

Definitions clause

'Appropriate representative' means any of the following:

(a) if employees are of a description in respect of which an independent union is recognised, representatives of that trade union; or
(b) in any other case, whichever of the following employee representa-tives that are chosen by the employer of:

(i) employee representatives appointed or elected by the employees otherwise than for the purposes of a transfer of undertakings transfer who have authority from these employees to receive information and to be consulted about the transfer on their benefit; or
(ii) employee representatives elected by them, for the purposes of the Transfer of Undertakings regulations in an election which satisfies the requirements of reg. 10A(1) of the Transfer of Undertakings Regulations.

'Compromise agreement' means an agreement that complies with the pro-visions set out in s. 203(3) of the Employment Rights Act 1996, in the form set out in Appendix 7 or in such other form as may from time to time require.

'Consultation information' means:

(a) the fact that the transfer is to take place;
(b) approximately when it is to take place;
(c) the reason for the transfer;
(d) the legal, economic and social implications for the transfer;
(e) the measures that the employer envisages it will take in relation to affected employees in connection with the transfer;
(f) where employees are to be transferred, the transferee must decide the measures it will take in relation to the transferring employees and the transferee will inform the transferor of any changes;
(g) a draft compromise agreement [*and/or*];
(h) any other information necessary to enable the parties to discharge their respective obligations under reg. 10 of the 1981 regulations.

'Consultation period' means a period of 28 calendar days during which the transferee, transferor and all appropriate representatives will consult in accordance with reg. 10 of the 1981 regulations or such longer period as may be required by the 1981 regulations.

'Employee' means any individual (who is not an objecting employee) who works under a contract of service who is employed by the transferor on or before the transfer date.

'Objecting employee' means an employee who indicates a desire to object to transferring to the transferee pursuant to reg. 5(4) of the 1981 regulations.

Draft compromise agreement

This agreement is made the [*date*] day of [*month*] 2002 between:

(1) ('the transferor') and
(2) ('the transferee') and
(3) ('the employee')

Preamble

There has been a transfer of an undertaking in accordance with the provisions of the Transfer of Undertakings (Protection of Employment) Regulations 1981 (the regulations) with the transferor conveyed to the transferee by lease the premises known as [*specify*] of [*address*] to the transferee.

The employee was assigned to the part transferred and indicated their consent to the transfer during a period of information and consultation.

The employee, therefore, transfers to the transferee in accordance with reg. 5 of the regulations.

The employee transfers to the transferee on the [*date*] day of [*month*] 2002 ('the transfer date').

The parties agree as follows:

1. That the employee acknowledges that he or she has not objected to transferring to the transferee nor is the identity of the transferee significant and to the employee's detriment.
2. The employee acknowledges that the transferee needs to take steps to harmonise terms and conditions of employment and these changes are as follows:

    (a) [*specify*]
    (b) [*specify*]

The contractual changes

3. The employee acknowledges that these changes were discussed during the information consultation period, which took place in accordance with reg. 10 of the regulations before the transfer date. The employee

also acknowledges that on transferring to the transferee the employee is not opposed to the above contractual changes being made to his or her terms and condition of employment.

4. In consideration of the transferee making changes to the employer's terms and condition of employment the transferee will pay to the employee the sum of £[*specify*] in full and final settlement of all claims which the employee may have against either the transferor or transferee arising from the employee's employment or its transfer from the transferor to the transferee on the transfer date or any contractual changes referred to in clause 2.

5. All sums paid under this agreement are paid without deduction of tax in accordance with the provisions of s. 148 of the Income Corporation Taxes Act 1988.

6. In consideration of receiving the payment referred to in clause 4 of this agreement the employee agrees that he or she has not at the date of signing the agreement and will not after signing the agreement pursue any claim in the employment tribunal, county or High Court in respect of the transfer from the transferor to the transferee or in respect of any of the contractual changes. The employee, therefore, agrees not to pursue any of the following complaints:

(a) a failure to inform and consult under reg. 10 of the TUPE regulations;

(b) a breach of contract in respect of the contractual changes referred to in clause 2;

(c) a claim under the Wages Act as emended by the Employment Rights Act 1996 in respect of the contractual changes;

(d) a claim for automatic and unfair dismissal under reg. 8 of the TUPE regulations in respect of the contractual changes; and/or

(e) a claim under reg. 5 of the TUPE regulations that the identity of the transferee is significant and to the employee's detriment;

(f) any other claim under the regulations in respect of the contractual changes.

7. The employee acknowledges that before signing this agreement he or she has received independent legal advice on the terms and effect of this agreement from a [a trade union representative/an independent solicitor [*name*]] and in particular its effects on the employee's ability to pursue his or her rights before an employment tribunal.

The conditions regulating compromise agreements under the Employment Rights Act 1996, s. 203 are certified in relation to this agreement.

Attestation

Signed by ....

Name ....

(1) ....

(2) ....

(3) ....

To be completed by the solicitor referred to in clause 7 above

1. I am a Solicitor of the Supreme Court of England & Wales holding a current Practising Certificate.
2. I have advised [*name*] as to the terms and effect of the Agreement and in particular its effect on his/her ability to pursue a claim in the employment tribunal.
3. There was in force, at the time of the advice, a policy of insurance covering the risk of a claim by [*name*] in respect of any loss arising from the consequence of that advice.

Date ....

Signature of solicitor ....

Index